FAITH CLINIC

VOLUME XXVIII
VIDEO GAMES EDITION

"You're Not Addicted to Gaming, You're Addicted to Escaping Your Own Life."

DR. PATRICIA S. TANNER

IBG Publications, Inc.

Published by I.B.G. Publications, Inc., a Power to Wealth Company

Web address: www.ibgpublications.com

admin@ibgpublications.com / 904-419-9810

Copyright, 2026 by Patricia S. Tanner

IBG Publications, Inc., Jacksonville, FL

ISBN: 978-1-971850-14-6

Tanner, Patricia S.

Faith Clinic, Volume XXVIII Video Games Edition- *"You're Not Addicted to Gaming, You're Addicted to Escaping Your Own Life."*

Printed in the United States of America.

DEDICATION

This book is dedicated to the ones who learned how to disappear without ever leaving the room.

To the players who mastered digital worlds but feel like beginners in their own lives. To the ones who stayed up all night conquering levels yet wake up each day feeling defeated. To the hearts that didn't choose escapism out of laziness, but out of exhaustion.

This is for the ones who found comfort behind a screen because life felt too loud, too heavy, too unpredictable… and too real.

To every person who has ever whispered, "I just need a break from my own life…"

I see you. More importantly, God sees you.

May these pages remind you that you were never created to hide in a world you can control, but to live boldly in the one God designed for you.

You are not weak for escaping.
You were overwhelmed.

But now… you're ready to return. Welcome back to your life.

With compassion and conviction,
Dr. Patricia S. Tanner
The Faith Doctor

TABLE OF CONTENTS

WELCOME TO THE FAITH CLINIC

Player One, You've Finally Checked In

Welcome to a place you probably didn't expect to end up in. You came here looking for help, but what you're walking into is an entire spiritual clinic designed specifically for people who are exhausted by real life and yet somehow deeply committed to battling digital monsters at two in the morning. This isn't the kind of clinic that hands you a prescription and sends you home with a polite pat on the back. No, this is the Faith Clinic, where your coping mechanisms get exposed, your hidden stress gets diagnosed, and the condition known as "I'll deal with my problems after this next round" gets treated with surgical honesty and holy humor.

You may not realize it yet, but checking into this clinic is already a sign of strength. It means something inside you knows it's time to stop pretending that avoiding real problems is the same as solving them. Somewhere beneath the constant noise of virtual battles and endless quests, there is a version of you that's tired of being tired, tired of running, tired of numbing out, and tired of pretending that gaming is "just a hobby," when deep down you know you've been using it as a life raft to float over things you don't want to feel. The Faith Clinic doesn't condemn you for that; it simply refuses to let you stay in the place that's been slowly draining your emotional health.

As you stand here at the door of this clinic, you're invited to set down the controller, silence the alerts, and take a moment to breathe without needing a digital world to regulate your emotions. You don't have to be defensive, embarrassed, or ashamed about why you've come. Life gets heavy. People disappoint you. Responsibilities pile up. Stress multiplies. And sometimes the fantasy of disappearing into someone else's universe feels safer than confronting your own. This clinic simply says, "You're human, and you deserve to heal." You deserve to be in real life, not just powerful in a virtual one.

Inside these pages, you'll be met with gentle truth, unapologetic clarity, and a whole lot of humor that will soften what your heart has been afraid to face. You'll learn why fictional worlds feel easier to conquer than your own struggles, why you feel so in control in a game but so overwhelmed in real life, and why your soul keeps buffering even when your internet doesn't. You'll discover that you're not just escaping into games, you're escaping from pain, discomfort, unresolved emotions, and unspoken fears. And you'll finally see that God is not trying to pull you away from the things you enjoy; He's trying to pull you back toward the life you abandoned because you didn't know how to live it without the escape.

So welcome to the Faith Clinic. There is no judgment here, only a journey you've needed far longer than you realized. You don't need to rage, quit life, withdraw from responsibilities, or keep running from the fears that chase you. You're here now, and that means something is already shifting. Healing starts the moment you decide to stop hiding. If you stay in this clinic long enough to hear the truth, feel the conviction, and embrace the transformation, you'll discover that you don't need an escape world to survive anymore. You only need courage, honesty, and a God who refuses to let you settle for half-alive living.

Take a deep breath. You've just taken your first real step back into your own life.

BEFORE WE BEGIN: PLEASE REMOVE YOUR HEADSET

Reality Has Been Trying to Talk to You for a While Now
Before we begin this journey, I need you to do something simple, but strangely more difficult than it sounds: take off your headset.

Not just physically, though yes, take it off, but mentally, emotionally, and spiritually. Detach from the world you've been hiding inside long enough to notice the one that has been waiting on you. Your headset has been serving as your doorway into a universe you can control, predict, and mute whenever you feel overwhelmed. And while that's great for entertainment, it's terrible for connection, presence, and healing.

Somewhere along the line, the headset became more than just an accessory. It became armor. It became insulation from reality. It became the safest way to tune out the emotions you weren't ready to deal with, the relationships that felt too complicated, the responsibilities that felt too heavy, and the stress that felt unmanageable. Every time life got loud, you covered your ears with digital comfort. Every time someone needed a conversation, you hit "mute." Every time your feelings start rising to the surface, you drown them out with in-game audio. Slowly, without even noticing, you trained your heart to depend on the headset more than on honesty, prayer, or emotional presence.

Taking off the headset feels uncomfortable because it requires vulnerability. It forces you to re-enter a world you don't always feel in control of. In the game, you choose your missions, you design your character, you respawn when things go wrong, and you regulate the volume of your problems. In real life, you don't have those same privileges. There's no volume slide for stress, no instant respawns for mistakes, no custom build for your weaknesses. But that doesn't mean real life is worse, it just means it's real, and real is where healing happens.

By removing your headset, you're choosing to stop filtering life through a buffer of entertainment and escape. You're choosing to hear yourself again, your thoughts, your frustrations, your needs, your longing for something deeper than dopamine hits and digital victories. You're choosing to hear the people around you, the ones who miss your presence even while your body is still in the room. Most importantly, you're choosing to hear God again, not through static, not through distraction, not through the noise of battle soundtracks, but through the stillness you've been avoiding.

This moment is sacred not because it's dramatic, but because it's honest. It admits that the headset served a purpose, but it has also become a barrier. And healing can't reach you through barriers you refuse to put down. Removing your headset is your way of saying, "I'm ready to show up." Not just in-game, but in life. Not just during victories, but during vulnerability. Not just for achievements, but for accountability. It is the first act of courage in this entire process.

So, before we go any further, take it off. Let your ears breathe. Let your mind decompress. Let the silence remind you that reality is not your enemy, it's your assignment. You don't have to be perfect to face it; you simply must be present. And the moment you remove that headset, you will realize that presence is something you are capable of, something you deserve, and something God has been patiently waiting for. Now that you're fully here, let's begin.

FAITH CLINIC INTAKE FORM

"Player Stats & Spiritual Symptoms"

Before we begin your healing journey, we need to get a clear picture of who you are, where you've been, and what battles you've been secretly fighting behind the screen. This intake form isn't meant to shame you, diagnose your humanity, or make you feel like you've failed at life.

It's simply here to help you understand yourself with a level of honesty you may not have practiced in a long time. Think of this as your character creation screen, except instead of choosing armor and abilities, you're choosing truth, awareness, and the willingness to confront the things you've been avoiding. Your honesty here will shape everything that follows, so take a deep breath, settle into yourself, and answer with the courage you keep thinking you don't have.

Player Name: _______________________________

This is where you write your actual name, not the one you hide behind online. We're not addressing "DragonSlayerX99," "Silent Rogue," "Night Elf Sniper," or whatever heroic identity you've built in your favorite game. We're speaking to *you*, the real person beneath the avatar, the one with feelings, memories, responsibilities, and a future worth investing in. Write the name that heaven knows, not the one your squad yells at when they need backup.

Level (Choose The One That Feels Honest)

You may think of yourself as a high-level player in the gaming world, but here in the real world, levels work differently. Are you someone who's just beginning to understand yourself? Are you a mid-level believer balancing faith and frustration? Are you a prestige-class avoider who has mastered the art of running from real-life responsibilities? Or are you the boss-level escape artist who can disappear emotionally faster than your Wi-Fi can drop a connection? None of these are indictments; they're simply checkpoints in your story. The goal isn't to judge your level, it's to learn where to begin your healing.

Current Life HP (Health Points)

This section asks you to be brutally honest about your emotional and spiritual vitality. Are you feeling strong and grounded? Are you surviving on autopilot? Are you at critically low energy, pretending you're fine while everything inside you feels like blinking red health? Is you one unresolved conversation away from crumbling? Your HP isn't just about your mood; it's about your internal capacity to feel, think, rest, connect, and show up. Naming your HP is the first step toward restoring it.

Spiritual Connection Status

Consider this your signal strength indicator. Are you connected to God, or do you feel like your spiritual life is lagging so badly you can't tell if He's speaking or if your soul is buffering? Are you like someone who stands in the room but is mentally miles away? Or have you been completely AFK, away from your faith, away from conviction, and away from the version of yourself who used to care? This isn't about guilt. It's about acknowledging connection loss so we can begin the reconnection process.

Emotional Inventory

This is where things get real. Have you been ignoring everything you feel because emotions seem too complicated to deal with? Have you become numb, functioning outwardly while your inner world feels shut down? Are you overwhelmed but pretending otherwise? Or have you been using gaming as emotional anesthesia, a quick and easy way to silence pain, stress, loneliness, or boredom? Your emotional inventory helps us identify what your heart has been carrying without support.

Primary Escape Route

Review your honest patterns. When life becomes too loud, do you run to games, social media, sleep, or the "I'm fine" mask you've been wearing for years? Escape isn't always intentional. Sometimes it becomes a habit you never realized you were forming. What matters now is identifying your go-to escape so we can understand why it feels safer than reality.

Boss Battle You Keep Avoiding

Write the thing you keep pushing off, the hard conversation, the unaddressed wound, the fear, the responsibility, the truth, the trauma, or the decision you've been postponing for months or years. Naming your boss battle doesn't make you weak; it makes you honest. And honesty is a weapon your healing depends on.

Side Quests Distracting You From Your Real Purpose

Just like in your favorite game, life is full of side quests that feel urgent but lead nowhere meaningful. Excessive gaming. Overcommitting. Overthinking. People-pleasing. Avoiding. Procrastinating. Say what's pulling your attention away from what matters. You might be surprised how much time you've spent leveling up the wrong parts of your life.

Emotions You've Muted With Gaming

List the feelings you've been drowning out with pixels and noise. Maybe it's loneliness. Maybe it's stress. Maybe it's heartbreak, disappointment, fear, or the exhaustion of pretending you're stronger than you feel. These emotions deserve acknowledgment, not punishment. The minute you write them down; you start reclaiming the power they've been holding.

What Healing Would Look Like For You

Describe your desired future. What does peace look like to you? What does presence feel like? What would it mean to live without needing to hide? What would your life look like if you didn't need a controller to cope, escape, or feel in control? Healing doesn't require perfection; it requires vision.

Signature: _______________________________________

Signing this form isn't a contract; it's a declaration. You're acknowledging that you've used fictional battles as a distraction from real ones, and you're choosing to face your life with courage. You're saying, "Yes, this is where I've been, but it won't be where I stay."

Reflections

____

____

____

____

____

____

____

____

____

📝 FAITH CLINIC INTAKE FORM

"Player Stats & Spiritual Symptoms"

Please fill out honestly. Lying only delays your healing.

Player Name: ______________________________

(Real name. Not your gamertag. "ShadowDragonSlayer89" won't help us.)

Level:
- ☐ Beginner at life
- ☐ Mid-level believer
- ☐ Prestige-class avoider
- ☐ Boss at running from emotions

Current Life HP (Health Points):
- ☐ Full
- ☐ Meh
- ☐ Critically low
- ☐ One emotional hit from fainting

Spiritual Connection Status:
- ☐ Online and stable
- ☐ Lagging
- ☐ Buffering
- ☐ Completely AFK from God

Emotional Inventory:
- ☐ Ignoring everything
- ☐ Numb but functioning

☐ Overwhelmed
☐ Using games as painkillers

Primary Escape Route:
☐ Gaming
☐ Scrolling
☐ Sleeping
☐ Pretending everything's fine
☐ All of the above

Boss Battle You Keep Avoiding: (Yes, that thing. Write it down.)

How Many Side Quests Are Distracting You From Your Real Purpose?

List the Emotions You've Muted With Gaming:

What Would Healing Look Like for You?

Please sign:

I agree to stop using fictional battles to avoid real ones.

Signature: _______________________________

⧗ THE WAITING ROOM

"Reality Will See You Shortly"

Welcome to the place that every patient tries to avoid but every healing journey absolutely requires: the waiting room. It may not look like much at first, just a quiet space with nothing flashing, vibrating, or leveling up, but don't let that simplicity fool you. This room is sacred. This is the first environment where you must sit with yourself without the digital noise that normally fills every empty space in your mind. For a long time, you've trained yourself to treat silence like an enemy and stillness like a threat. But for the next few moments, you're going to experience something different: the luxury of being fully present with your own soul.

In this waiting room, there are no controllers to grip when emotions get uncomfortable, no achievement notifications to give you a quick hit of validation, and no teammates yelling instructions through your headset, drowning out the sound of your own heart. There is just you, the version of you that exists when no game is buffering your fears, blocking your thoughts, or numbing your stress. You may feel a little restless. You may be tempted to reach for your phone. You may experience a sudden, dramatic urge to reorganize your backpack, check imaginary notifications, or convince yourself you left the oven on. That is what happens when a person who has been living at maximum stimulation suddenly meets stillness. Do not panic. You are not malfunctioning. You are awakening.

This room represents the gap between your escape world and your real world, the space where you transition from running to reflecting. And although you may not love this part, it's one of the most important steps in your healing. Waiting rooms force you to confront the truth that you've been avoiding you don't need a controller to survive your reality. You don't need a headset to hide your emotions. You don't need a fictional universe to feel safe. You just need to stay still long enough to notice the things you've been outrunning, your fatigue, your fears, your loneliness, your dreams, your regrets, your need for purpose, and your deep desire for connection.

This is also the place where you begin to sense something you can't feel when you're escaping: the gentle pull of God calling you back to yourself. He speaks differently in the waiting room. His voice isn't competing with explosions, battle music, or character selection screens. It speaks in the quiet thoughts you push away, the emotions you've muted, the heaviness you haven't named, and the hope you didn't realize was still buried inside you. The waiting room is where God whispers the things you've been too distracted to hear: "You're overwhelmed. You're tired. You're hurting. And you don't have to carry this alone."

As you sit here, notice the weight of your own presence. Notice how strange but peaceful this unfiltered moment feels. Notice the difference between stillness and stagnation, one heals, the other harms. Notice that the world didn't fall apart without your constant distraction. Notice that you are still breathing, still valuable, still wanted, and still capable of showing up for your own life. Healing requires your participation. Restoration requires your honesty. And both require moments exactly like this, quiet, unhurried, and fully awake.

So, take this moment seriously. Sink into the chair. Let your hands relax. Let your mind stop sprinting. Let your emotions catch up to your body. You are not trapped here; you are being prepared. You are not being punished by waiting; you are being stabilized. Life has been trying to call your name for a while now, but you've been logged out, distracted, and emotionally unavailable. This waiting room is the place where you reconnect with reality long enough to hear it call you again.

Reality will see you shortly. And for the first time in a long time… You're going to be ready for it.

🎫 FAITH CLINIC WRISTBAND

"Healing Mode: ON"
(Issued Upon Admission, Do Not Remove Until Wholeness Is Completed)

PATIENT IDENTIFICATION WRISTBAND

Patient Name: ________________________________

(Your real name. Not your gamertag.)

Clinic: FAITH CLINIC, VIDEO GAMES EDITION

Status: ACTIVE PATIENT

Condition: Chronic Escapism / Reality Avoidance Syndrome

Treatment Plan: Presence • Honesty • Healing • Holy Spirit Intervention

<u>Restrictions:</u>
- No emotional disappearing
- No AFK from real life
- No rage quitting your responsibilities
- Limited access to digital anesthesia

<u>**Wristband Code:**</u> HC–VG–001 (*Healing Clinic: Video Games: Patient 001*)

Mode: ◍ **HEALING MODE: ON** (Processing… Updating… Stabilizing…)

PATIENT INSTRUCTIONS

Keep this wristband on as long as you:
- feel tempted to escape reality
- want to disappear into a fictional world
- feel your emotions rising and want to numb out

- start drifting away from God, people, and purpose
- feel overwhelmed and tempted to go spiritually offline

This wristband is your reminder that you are *not* running away anymore. You are present. You are here. You are healing.

EMERGENCY NOTE

If you feel the urge to:
- binge-game to avoid emotions
- go mentally AFK
- mute your feelings under noise
- detach from real conversations
- disappear into a fantasy world

STOP. LOOK AT THIS BAND. BREATHE. You are in the middle of a healing process. Don't check out now, God is doing something in you.

AUTHORIZED BY:
Faith Clinic Medical & Spiritual Division
Dr. Truth • Nurse Conviction • Technician Holy Spirit *Your healing team from the moment you walked through these pages.*

FINAL REMINDER
This wristband is not a punishment, it's your proof that you are reclaiming your life, one honest moment at a time.

HEALING MODE: ON
No logging out. No disconnecting. No disappearance. You're staying plugged into **your** life now.

THE DOCTOR'S ORDERS

Prescription for Patients Struggling With Chronic Digital Escapism, Emotional AFK Episodes, and Reality Avoidance.

PATIENT NAME: ___________________

DATE: ______________________________

CASE NUMBER: VG–HC–2025

(*Video Games: Healing Clinic*)

PRIMARY DIAGNOSIS:

Acute Reality Avoidance Triggered by Excessive Gaming Used as Emotional Escape.
Your symptoms include:
• difficulty facing real-life responsibilities
• emotional buffering through gaming
• spiritual lag
• avoidance of difficult conversations
• and a tendency to choose digital battles over personal healing

But the good news?
None of these symptoms are terminal, except for running from your own growth.

TREATMENT PLAN:

3. *LIMIT ESCAPE, NOT ENJOYMENT.*
You are not required to quit gaming. You *are* required to stop using gaming to avoid your life. Set time limits. Stick to them. Real life deserves time too.

2. DAILY "RECONNECT" CHECK-IN, 10 MINUTES MINIMUM.
No screens. No noise. No characters, missions, or quests. Just you, God, and your thoughts. Let your emotions load without interference.

3. FACE ONE REAL-LIFE "BOSS BATTLE" A WEEK.

This could be:
• a hard conversation
• a task you've been avoiding
• a personal goal
• or an emotion you've muted
You don't need to conquer all your battles, just the next one.

4. REPLACE ESCAPE WITH EXPRESSION.

When you feel overwhelmed, don't vanish into a screen.
Instead:
• journal
• pray
• breathe
• talk to someone safe
• step outside
Your feelings aren't glitches, they're data.

5. ESTABLISH HEALTHY XP (EXPERIENCE POINTS).

Track small wins like:
• being present
• showing up
• finishing a task
• talking instead of avoiding
• praying instead of escaping
Every victory counts toward your healing level.

6. WEEKLY "SOUL UPDATE" WITH GOD.

You don't need a headset to hear Him. Just honesty. Tell Him what you're avoiding, what you're afraid of, and where you feel stuck. Healing uploads best when the connection is real.

7. MAINTAIN YOUR FAITH CLINIC WRISTBAND.

Before you hit "Start" on your favorite game, glance at your band and ask: **Am I escaping… or am I just relaxing?** If it's escape, pause. If it's relaxation, enjoy. Healing starts with awareness.

8. PRACTICE "CONTROL ALT DELETE" ON TOXIC HABITS.

Control your thoughts. Alter your behavior. Delete your excuses. And restart your day with grace instead of guilt.

9. KEEP YOUR SPIRITUAL BATTERY CHARGED.

Scripture. Prayer. Rest. Community. Your soul cannot run on low power mode while your gaming skills stay at 100%.

10. REMEMBER: YOU CAN'T RESPAWN IN REAL LIFE.

Make choices that support healing, wholeness, and mental stability. No rage quitting your own journey.

Reflections

____

____

____

____

____

____

____

____

FOLLOW-UP APPOINTMENT:

Your next chapter.
(Healing is mandatory. Escapism is optional.)

AUTHORIZED BY:
Faith Clinic Medical Board Dr. Truth, Lead Physician
Nurse Conviction, Emotional Care Unit Technician Holy Spirit,
Transformation Department
Signature: _______________________________________

[sos] EMERGENCY AFK CARD

"When You Feel Like Escaping Again"
(Pull this card out when you feel the urge to go mentally offline.)

PATIENT NAME: _______________________________________
CASE ID: AFK–001
STATUS: At Risk for Escapism Episode

⚠ EMERGENCY SYMPTOMS CHECKLIST

If you are experiencing ANY of the following, pause before
disappearing:

- sudden desire to avoid emotions
- urge to hide in a game instead of handling reality
- heaviness, numbness, or emotional overload
- mental shutdown
- desire to mute people, conversations, or responsibilities
- overwhelming stress that makes gaming feel like the only escape
- thoughts like "I can't deal with this right now"
- temptation to go AFK from life

If one or more apply, **STOP.** This is a moment of decision, not
defeat.

⚕ __STEP 1__: TAKE A BREATH, RESET YOUR SYSTEM

Breathe in deeply. Hold it for three seconds. Let it out slowly. Repeat until your shoulders drop and your thoughts stop sprinting. Your nervous system needs grounding before your mind runs to escape.

💬 __STEP 2__: SAY THIS OUT LOUD (OR IN YOUR HEART)

"I don't have to run. I don't have to hide. I can face this. God is with me. And I am stronger than this moment." Your words create your atmosphere. Choose ones that stabilize you.

✸ __STEP 3__: ASK YOURSELF THE REAL QUESTION

"Am I playing to relax, or to disappear?" If the answer leans toward disappearing, this is your sign: **Don't go offline. Stay present.**

⌨ __STEP 4__: NAME WHAT YOU'RE FEELING

Your emotions can't heal if they stay unspoken. Write or say: "I feel _________________________. And it matters." Naming the emotion reduces its power.

📞 __STEP 5__: CONTACT YOUR REALITY ANCHOR

Choose one:
- pray
- journal
- talk to someone safe
- step outside
- drink water
- take a five-minute break without screens

Escaping won't solve it. Presence will.

💡 __STEP 6__: REMEMBER THIS TRUTH

You don't need a virtual world to survive the real one. You just need honesty, breath, and God's help. Every time you stay present instead of disappearing, you level up in real life.

⚖ EMERGENCY AFFIRMATION

"I refuse to go AFK from my own healing."

AUTHORIZED BY: Faith Clinic Crisis Response Unit"
• Dr. Truth
• Nurse Conviction
• Technician Holy Spirit **Healing Hotline (Internal): PRAY–NOW**

Reflections

INTRODUCTION

"The Escape That Almost Erased You"

There comes a moment in every gamer's life when you realize you didn't simply pick up a controller; the controller picked you up. What started as something fun, innocent, and entertaining slowly transformed into something else entirely. It became a portal. A hiding place. A numbing agent. A world-within-a-world where your problems couldn't reach you, your emotions couldn't overwhelm you, and your responsibilities couldn't find you. It offered a sense of control you didn't feel in real life, a sense of progression you couldn't always measure in your daily decisions, and a sense of validation that didn't depend on the approval of people who have disappointed you.

Gaming didn't become dangerous because it was "bad." It became dangerous because it became *comfortable*. And comfort, when used as escape, always comes with a cost. If you're honest, you didn't come to this book because someone forced you. You came because something inside you whispered that maybe, just maybe, you've been slipping away from yourself without meaning to. You've been logging into fictional worlds consistently while logging out of your real one gradually. People around you may see presence, but you know you've been *functionally absent*. They see you sitting on the couch, but emotionally you're miles away. They talk to you, but you're mentally muted. You're not irresponsible; you're exhausted.

You're not detached; you're overwhelmed. You're not gaming too much just because it's fun, you're gaming too much because it's **safe**.

Let's tell the truth you've been avoiding: **You're not addicted to gaming; you're addicted to escaping your own life.** There's something in your real world that hurts, drains you, bores you, disappoints you, or scares you. Maybe it's responsibilities that feel heavier than your emotional strength. Maybe it's memories you don't want to revisit, feelings you don't want to feel, conversations you don't want to have, or pressures you don't know how to articulate. Maybe life has been unfair, unpredictable, overwhelming, or painfully ordinary, and the game gave you the excitement, control, or progress you could not find anywhere else. You didn't run from your life because you're weak. You ran because no one taught you how to face it without crumbling. And that's where the Faith Clinic steps in.

This book is not an anti-gaming manifesto. It will not tell you to throw away your console, burn your PC, uninstall every game you love, and take a vow of boredom for the rest of your life. Absolutely not. Gaming itself is not the enemy. The real enemy is *the escape*. The emotional disconnect. The quiet disappearance. This is innocent when your soul screams for attention, but you drown it in pixels and soundtracks. The moments when God is trying to speak to you, but you can't hear Him through the noise of another fight, another mission, another quest you didn't need but desperately wanted. The moments when real life start buffering because your heart has logged out.

This book is for the part of you that knows something is missing, not in your gaming experience but in yourself. You feel it when the game ends and the silence hits. You feel it when you turn off the console and the heaviness returns. You feel it when you try to sleep but your mind is restless. You feel it when someone asks how you're doing and you don't have the energy to make up a believable lie.

You feel it when you want more out of life, but you're too drained to pursue it. You feel it when God feels distant, even though He's been trying to get your attention in the moments you've escaped the most.

The Faith Clinic exists to pull you gently but firmly, back into your own life. It will help you understand why gaming became your hiding place, why escapism feels easier than facing reality, why your emotions feel too loud to handle, and why your spiritual life has felt muted, laggy, or offline. It will walk you through the deeper layers of your heart, the ones you've been protecting through avoidance, and reveal the truth that healing isn't found in escaping your life but in reclaiming it with courage and guidance.

You will learn that you don't need a respawn button to fix your mistakes; you need presence. You don't need power-ups to overcome your struggles; you need clarity. You don't need a fictional world to feel alive; you need a restored relationship with yourself, with others, and with God.

This introduction is your checkpoint. Your first step back into your storyline. Your invitation to stop hiding and start healing. You don't have to stop gaming. You just must stop disappearing. And this book will show you how. Welcome, Player One. Your healing has officially begun.

Chapter 1:

Respawning Isn't Real Life, Sorry, Player One

Symptom: Avoiding consequences, conversations, and adulting.

There's a moment in almost every video game when the screen fades to black, your character collapses dramatically, and the words **"RESPAWN AVAILABLE"** flash with comforting confidence. In that split second, you're reminded of one of gaming's most seductive features: mistakes don't cost you anything permanent. You can fall off the cliff, jump too soon, choose the wrong enemy, run out of health, or get ambushed by something you didn't see coming, and still, all it takes is one button to bring you back. No rebuilding. No consequences. No lingering embarrassment. No long-term damage. Respawn, retry, repeat.

But here is the part you don't like to admit out loud: you've gotten so used to respawning in games that you've started expecting it in real life. You've become conditioned to believe you can make any impulsive decision, postpone any responsibility, avoid any uncomfortable  conversation, or disappear during any emotional moment, and then somehow "respawn" into a clean slate like nothing happened. You subconsciously hope that people will forget what you didn't do, overlook what you didn't say, or magically reset the expectations you ignored. You want the real world to follow the same logic as the digital one, where consequences are temporary, discomfort is optional, and every mistake comes with an instant do-over.

But real life is not a game, and this is where the trouble begins. In real life, every avoided conversation builds tension. Every postponed responsibility grows heavier. Every emotion you suppress becomes more complicated. Every unspoken need becomes harder to articulate. Every moment you disappear affects someone else's stability. And every time you try to "respawn" from an emotionally hard moment, you discover that life doesn't refresh your health bar or reset your problems. It just waits, patiently, quietly, and consistently. The things you avoided don't vanish; they multiply, deepening the ache you were trying to escape.

Yet the pull of escapism is strong. Games make you feel competent, powerful, and in control. Real life, on the other hand, can make you feel overwhelmed, underprepared, and emotionally unequipped. It's no wonder you retreat into environments where you can respawn as often as necessary. But the real danger is this: *the more you rely on respawning in games, the less resilient you become in life.* Resilience doesn't grow in fantasy worlds. It grows, the place where things don't reset, feelings don't disappear, and you don't get unlimited chances to redo what you avoided.

This chapter exists to call you out gently but truthfully. You've developed a habit of running from anything that threatens your sense of control. You escape difficult moments instead of resolving them. Your mute discomfort instead of processing it. You disappear when emotions get too loud instead of learning how to handle them. You tell yourself, "I'll deal with it later," even though later rarely comes. And every time you choose to escape engagement, you lose a little more of your real life while gaining nothing but temporary relief.

But here's the good news, and I promise there's good news: your habit of avoiding it doesn't mean you're broken. It means you've been coping the only way you knew how. Gaming became a survival strategy, a refuge, a safe hiding place from the parts of life you felt unprepared to face. And while that escape may have protected you during seasons when reality felt too heavy to carry, it's now keeping you from the growth, stability, and emotional maturity you desperately need.

This chapter will gently pull back the layers of your avoidance and expose the truth beneath it: *you don't fear life, you fear hurting again.* You're not afraid of responsibility; you're afraid of failing.

You're not afraid of connection; you're afraid of disappointment. You're not afraid of emotional presence; you're afraid of being seen. And gaming gave you a world where none of those fears exist.

But healing begins the moment you acknowledge that real life will not offer you a respawn button, just grace, growth, and the chance to do better today than you did yesterday. God doesn't give you do-overs; He gives you transformation. He doesn't erase the past; He redeems it. He doesn't reset your life; He restores what you bring to Him honestly.

So let this chapter be your first step out of escapism and into engagement. No more trying to respawn from the emotions you don't want to feel, the conversations you don't want to have, or the responsibilities you don't want to own. You don't need endless do-overs. You need courage, presence, and a willingness to stand in your life instead of running from it. You're not here to respawn. You're here to return, fully, honestly, and bravely, to yourself.

Teaching: Why you'd rather reset your problems than resolve them.

The idea of respawning in games feels comforting because it offers what life rarely does: instant recovery without lingering consequences. In a digital world, your character can fail spectacularly fall off cliffs, get ambushed, lose battles, make poor decisions, and yet within seconds, you are given a fresh start. There is no shame attached, no  judgment waiting, no emotional residue. Just a clean slate and permission to try again. This creates a powerful psychological loop where mistakes feel temporary, failure feels harmless, and starting over feels easy. Eventually, the brain begins associating "resetting" with safety, and that becomes a dangerous expectation you subconsciously carry into real life.

The concept of respawning doesn't exist. When you avoid a conversation, it doesn't fade to black and rewrite itself. When you ignore responsibilities, they don't reset themselves overnight. When you walk away from tension, unresolved emotions don't magically dissolve. Life is cumulative, not cyclical. Every unsaid thing builds upon the last unsaid thing. Every avoidance grows roots. Every delayed responsibility gain weight. Every postponed emotion evolves into something heavier. But when you're conditioned by games to believe  you'll always get a clean slate, you start avoiding anything that threatens your sense of control, as if avoiding discomfort will somehow reset it.

At the core of this pattern is not laziness or irresponsibility, as people might assume. It's fear. The desire to "respawn" comes from the fear of making irreversible mistakes. You want the safety of starting over because you're terrified of being wrong, being misunderstood, or facing consequences you don't know how to handle. The digital world lets you experiment without risk, but the real world demands vulnerability. In life, when you speak honestly, things might shift. When you show up fully, someone might see you. When you take responsibility, you must face the results. The fear of those unknown outcomes becomes so overwhelming that escape feels easier than engagement.

There's also the emotional component. Video games offer structured, measurable growth. You see progress in the form of levels, upgrades, achievements, and stats. Real life offers no such clarity. You can work on yourself and still feel like nothing is moving. You can show up in your relationships and still experience conflict. You can try to grow spiritually and still feel stuck. Because life doesn't provide immediate feedback, your mind reaches for environments where growth is obvious, progress is rewarded, and mistakes don't cost you anything. A game gives you validation; life gives you challenge. And for someone who feels overwhelmed or unprepared, validation becomes addictive.

But beneath the psychological patterns lies a spiritual truth that is even deeper: **God never designed you to live life through the lens of escape.** Every attempt to respawn your emotions, restart your responsibilities, or reset your relationships is an attempt to protect yourself from the vulnerability required for healing. But healing does not happen in shortcuts. Wholeness is not achieved through avoidance. Growth does not come from restarting problems; it comes from walking through them with wisdom and courage. God is not in the business of offering respawns; He is in the business of offering redemption. Redemption doesn't erase your past, it transforms it.

The habit of expecting life to reset comes from a misunderstanding  of grace. Many people treat grace like a respawn button, a way to erase the consequences of avoidance or emotional absence. But grace isn't a reset; it's an invitation. Grace says, "Bring me your mess, and I will help you rebuild," not "Pretend the mess never happened." Grace strengthens you for real life, not fictional escape routes. And healing requires you to stop waiting for life to reset and start learning how to respond differently.

The truth is the very thing you're trying to avoid is the very thing God wants to use to grow you. The conversations you avoid are the ones that would strengthen your relationships. The emotions you mute are the pathways to your true self. The responsibilities you dodge are the areas where your discipline and identity would thrive. Escaping delays your growth but facing what you've been avoiding activates it. Healing requires presence. It requires honesty. It requires the willingness to stop respawning and start responding.

This teaching section is not here to shame you but to help you understand the psychology behind your patterns and the spiritual transformation you're invited into. You don't have to master real life in one day. You don't need to go from avoidance to bravery overnight. You simply need to acknowledge that real life cannot and will not, offer you respawns. It offers you something better: the opportunity to grow in endurance, truth, maturity, and wisdom. And once you begin embracing those things, you'll realize that you don't need to run to fictional worlds to feel strong. You can become strong on your own.

💊 FAITH PRESCRIPTION

You show up for it or not. Your prescription is not a list of restrictions but a path toward reclaiming your role in your own story. For this week, and every week until the instinct to avoid begins to loosen its grip, you are instructed to practice intentional presence. Intentional presence means noticing the moment you want to escape and choosing instead to stay long enough to understand what you're feeling. When you reach for a controller out of habit, pause and ask yourself, "What am I trying to avoid?" Awareness is not punishment; it is power.

Another part of your prescription is to take one real-life action that you normally avoid. It does not have to be dramatic or heavy. It can be as simple as returning a text you've been putting off, completing a task you've been procrastinating, or admitting out loud that you're overwhelmed. The point is not to become perfect at responsibility but to disrupt the cycle of avoidance. Every small action is a form  of healing. Every act of courage breaks the pattern of escape. Consider this your antidote to emotional respawning: do one thing in real life that pushes your storyline forward. Growth does not happen automatically; it happens intentionally.

Additionally, your spirit needs nourishment. Just as a game needs energy, updates, and stable connection to run well, so does your soul. Set aside ten minutes daily, even if they feel inconvenient, to sit with God and tell Him the truth. Be honest: "I don't know how to deal with things without escaping." God is not offended by your confession; He is invited into it. The more you talk to Him; the less intimidating life becomes. You are not praying to impress Him; you are praying to reconnect with the One who strengthens you for what you keep running from.

Finally, your prescription includes grace. Not the cheap, "let me escape again" kind of grace, but the strengthening kind that gives you courage to face the things you once avoided. Grace is not erasing your problems; it's empowering you to approach them differently. So, take your prescription seriously. You don't need a respawn button. You need truth, courage, and the willingness to stay present long enough to heal.

🕊 HOLY SPIRIT CONSULT

"Let Me Strengthen You Where You Keep Shutting Down."

In this consultation, the Holy Spirit speaks into the exact places you've been trying to reset instead of repairing. If you could hear His voice without the noise of your escape, you would know He has never shamed you for running, He has simply waited for the moment  you got tired of running. He says to you, "I know why you hide. I know what scares you. I know the weight you've been carrying in secret. And I am not here to expose your weakness; I am here to empower you in it. You've been trying to avoid life because you believed you had to face it alone, but you were never meant to fight without Me."

The Holy Spirit continues, "Every time you feel the urge to escape, that is not failure, it is a signal. It is your heart asking for help.

Instead of running to a screen, run to Me. I can handle the fear you don't want to feel. I can strengthen the places where you are tired. I can calm the thoughts that feel too loud. I can guide you through the conversations you don't want to have, and I can give you peace in the moments where you feel emotionally overloaded. You don't need a reset; you need reassurance. You don't need to respawn; you need renewal."

He reminds you that real transformation doesn't come from avoiding but from surrendering. "Give Me the part of your life you keep trying to escape. Give Me the moment you feel overwhelmed. Give Me your anxiety, your fear, your frustration, and your exhaustion. I am not afraid of your feelings. I am not annoyed by your struggles. I am here to walk with you into the very places you've been running from. Let Me show you that you don't need to escape to survive, you need My presence to thrive."

This consult ends with a divine truth*:* the strength you need is already available. The courage you keep trying to manufacture is already within reach. The peace you crave is not found in escaping your life, it's found in inviting the Holy Spirit into it.

GUIDED PRAYER

"Lord, Help Me Stop Running From the Life You Gave Me."
Heavenly Father, I come to You with honesty, even though honesty feels uncomfortable. I confess that I have been running from things I don't know how to handle. I have used distraction, entertainment, and escape as ways to avoid facing my feelings, responsibilities, and fears. I have treated respawning like a solution, when it has only pushed my healing further away. Today, I ask for Your help, real help, the kind that meets me where I am and strengthens me where I feel weak.

Lord, teach me how to stay present. When I feel overwhelmed, I remind myself that I am not alone. When I want to shut down emotionally, whisper to my heart that You can hold the feelings I'm scared to face. When I want to disappear, anchor me to Your peace. Give me courage to face the things I have avoided. Give me clarity to see what needs my attention. Give me strength to show up in my own life without hiding in fictional ones.

Holy Spirit, I invite You into the moments where I feel the urge to escape. Interrupt my patterns. Redirect my thoughts. Replace my fear with Your comfort and my avoidance with Your guidance. Help me choose honesty over hiding and healing over escape. Show me how to rebuild the parts of my life I have neglected. And remind me that I don't need endless restarts, I need Your grace to move forward.

God, I surrender the need to escape. I surrender the temptation to shut down. I surrender the fear of facing my own life. Lead me toward healing, stability, and wholeness. And thank You for loving me even in the moments when I tried to run. In Jesus 'name, amen.

REFLECTION PAGES

Use this reflection page to process the deeper layers of what you've read. Take your time. Be honest. Be gentle with yourself.

1. What emotions do you try to avoid most often?
Write about the feelings you try to escape, stress, sadness, anxiety, fear, loneliness, frustration. Why do they feel it is easier to run from to face?

____

____

____

____

____

____

____

2. What is one responsibility you've been "respawning" from instead of resolving?
Identify something you keep postponing. Why has it been hard to address?

____

____

____

____

____

____

3. Are there conversations you've avoided out of fear of conflict or vulnerability?
Write what those conversations are and how avoidance has affected you.

____

____

____

____

____

____

____

____

4. In what moments do you feel the strongest urge to escape?
Describe the triggers. Is it pressure? Emotional overload? Boredom?
Fear of disappointing others?

____

____

____

____

____

____

**5. If you stopped trying to respawn and started responding, how
would your life begin to change?**
Imagine your future self. What does that version of you look like?

____

____

____

____

____

____

____

____

6. What would courage look like for you this week?
List one action you can take that aligns with presence instead of avoidance.

____

____

____

____

____

____

____

7. How can you remind yourself that God is with you when you want to run?
Write the truth you need for the moments when escape feels easier than healing. Take your time with this. These questions aren't meant to overwhelm you; they are meant to **reconnect you** with the parts

of your life you've been distant from. Healing doesn't require perfection; it requires presence.

Additional Reflections

Chapter 2:

You Didn't Escape the Game...
The Game Escaped You

Symptom: When entertainment becomes emotional anesthesia.

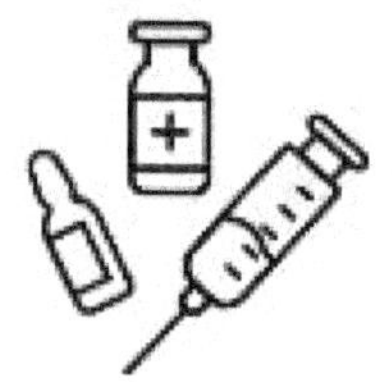

There is a moment in every gamer's life when the shift happens, slowly, quietly, almost invisibly. First, you pick up a controller because you enjoy it. It's fun. It's entertainment. It is a way to unwind after a long day. But over time, without realizing it, the purpose of gaming starts to change. What used to be something you ran *to* becomes something you run *into*. Not because the graphics improved or the storyline deepened but because your life felt heavier than usual, your emotions felt louder than normal, and the game became the only place where the noise inside you went silent.

Before you knew it, entertainment wasn't entertainment anymore. It became **emotional anesthesia**, a way to numb your mind, mute your heart, and drown out whatever you didn't want to feel. You didn't escape into the game; the game escaped into you. It crawled underneath your frustration, your exhaustion, your loneliness, and your stress, and it promised relief in exchange for your presence. Not healing. Just relief. The kind that wears off the second you turn off the console.

Gaming stopped being a hobby the moment it became the quickest way to shut down the emotional system inside you that was trying to communicate something important. You weren't trying to hide. You were trying to breathe. But somewhere along the way, you forgot that real breathing requires presence, not escape. So, you kept reaching for the controller, not to play, but to pause your own life.

Emotional anesthesia doesn't always feel dramatic. It usually feels like subtle avoidance: "I'll play for a bit and then deal with things later." Later just never came. The game became your buffer, your sedation, the cushion between you and the things you didn't want to confront. When emotions rise, you are gamed. When stress hits, your games. When loneliness crept in, you gamed. When disappointment stung, you gamble. The screen became your quiet place, your comfort zone, your emotional dimmer switch.

But emotional anesthesia has a cost. It numbs everything, not just the pain. It numbs joy. It numbs connection. It numbs clarity. It numbs creativity. It numbs purpose. It numbs the ability to feel alive in your own life. People think you're zoning out, but they don't understand you're self-soothing with the only method that doesn't ask you to talk, explain, or be vulnerable. Gaming doesn't demand emotional availability. It doesn't require conversation. It doesn't ask why you're sad or what triggered you today. It doesn't challenge you to grow, reflect, or heal. It just offers instant escape, numbness on demand.

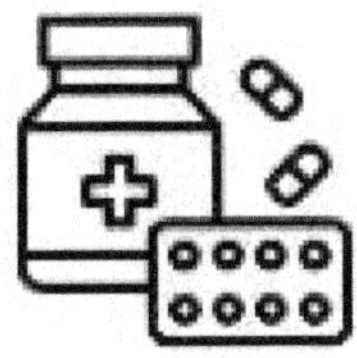

But here is the truth that you've been avoiding numbness is not healing. It is a pause button on pain. And eventually, that pain starts buffering again the moment life resumes. When entertainment becomes your anesthetic, the game may provide temporary relief, but it also prevents long-term restoration. It offers comfort without correction. Escape without clarity. Distraction without direction.

The symptom of emotional anesthesia looks like this: You're not gaming because the game is exciting, you're gaming because your emotions feel threatening. You're not playing because you're bored, you're playing because your heart is tired. You're not logging in for fun; you're logging in for silence. You're not escaping your life you're escaping your feelings.

The longer this pattern continues, the more your emotional endurance weakens. What used to be manageable suddenly feels unbearable. What used to be a small inconvenience suddenly feels like a major battle. What used to be a simple conversation with someone now feels like a threat to your emotional safety. You've been numbing instead of navigating, sedating instead of surrendering, avoiding instead of acknowledging. And while gaming protected you from emotional overwhelm for a season, it also robbed you of the practice you needed to build resilience. You haven't been weak, you've been numb. And numbness makes everything feel heavier when the anesthetic wears off.

But here's the good news: God doesn't shame you for how you coped. He simply invites you into something better. Something sustainable. Something real. Something healing. He wants to show you that your emotions aren't threats; they're signals. They're not meant to be silenced; they're meant to be understood. They're not your enemies; they're your internal indicators that something inside you needs attention.

You didn't escape the game. The game escaped the boundaries you once had around your heart. But the moment you recognize the shift; you regain the power to change it. And now, you're here — in the Faith Clinic, not because you failed, but because you're finally ready to feel again.

TEACHING

You Didn't Escape the Game… The Game Escaped You

The transformation from "fun" to "escape" happens slowly, quietly, and almost invisibly. The shift is rarely dramatic. You don't wake up one day and declare, "Today, I shall avoid all my emotions with a controller." Instead, it starts with a stressful day. A disappointment you don't want  to think about. A conversation that drained you. A pressure you didn't know how to name. You tell yourself, "Let me play for a little while to unwind."

And for a moment, it works. Your heartbeat slows. Your mind quiets. Your emotions settle. The noise inside you fades. The world becomes manageable again. And at that moment, the game offers you something that feels like peace, even though it's just silence.

But over time, that silence becomes addictive, not because the game is so extraordinary, but because life feels so loud. What once was entertainment slowly transformed into anesthesia. You aren't playing to enjoy yourself anymore; you're playing to avoid yourself. You're not logging 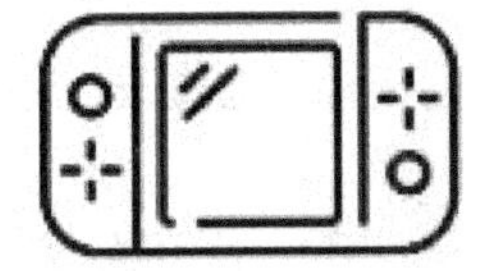 in because you're excited. You're logging in because you're overwhelmed. You're not chasing fun; you're chasing numbness. And numbness is powerful because it promises relief without requiring vulnerability.

But numbness has a dark side: it doesn't just numb the pain; it numbs your ability to process it. It numbs your joy. It numbs your clarity. It numbs your connection with others. It numbs your emotional stamina. And eventually, it numbs your relationship with God. When you use gaming as anesthesia, you silence your inner world instead of understanding it. You mute your heart instead of healing it. You disconnect from your feelings instead of dealing with them honestly.

The teaching in this chapter is simple but uncomfortable: *The game didn't take over your life. You handed it your emotional steering wheel.* Not because you're irresponsible, but because you're hurting. Not because you lack discipline, but because you lack support. Not because you don't care, but because you don't know how to cope. The game became your emotional "off switch" the quickest way to turn down the intensity inside you. But the more you use it to numb, the more your emotional capacity shrinks.

Suddenly, things you used to handle with ease feel like devastation. Simple tasks feel overwhelming. Normal responsibilities feel impossible. Everyday emotions feel catastrophic. Not because you're weak, but because your emotional muscles haven't been exercised. You've been sedating them, not strengthening them.

God is not angry that you found something that made you feel safe. But He also knows you deserve more than a life lived on mute. He knows you deserve boundaries, not numbing. Presence, not escape. Healing, not sedation. And that kind of healing starts with recognizing that entertainment turned into anesthesia the moment you started using it to avoid your life.

This chapter calls you back to yourself, not to shame you, but to restore you. You didn't lose control. You just lose awareness. And awareness is how you get your life back.

💊 FAITH PRESCRIPTION

"Replace Numbing With Naming."
Your prescription for this chapter begins with a practice that feels  deceptively simple but is deeply transformational: name what you're feeling before you play. Every time you feel the urge to disappear into a game, pause long enough to ask, "What am I trying to escape?" You don't need a perfect answer. You don't need to write a paragraph. Just name the emotion, frustration, sadness, anxiety, loneliness, boredom, overwhelm. Naming reduces the power of numbing. It transforms avoidance into awareness, and awareness into healing.

Next, schedule intentional gaming times. Not as punishment, but as boundaries. When gaming has no boundaries, it becomes anesthesia. When it has structure, it becomes enjoyable again. Choose blocks in your day where gaming is something you do for fun, not something you use for escape. This retrains your brain to seek pleasure, not sedation. You're not quitting gaming; you're reclaiming it.

Third, take a five-minute grounding break before you play. No screens. No noise. Just five minutes of breathing, acknowledging your feelings, and reconnecting with your body. Your nervous system needs grounding before reaching for digital sedation. Those five minutes will tell you whether you're playing to relax or playing to disappear.

Fourth, schedule one emotionally honest action each day, something small but real. Send the message you've been avoiding. Wash the dish you've been pretending doesn't exist. Admit yourself to yourself that you're tired. Drink water. Step outside. You don't need dramatic change. You need small engagements that remind your brain that life won't kill you if you'represent.

Lastly, invite God into your emotional waves. Say, "Lord, I don't want to escape this moment. Help me face it." You will be shocked at how much that one sentence shifts your response. You're not fighting alone. You're healing with support.

☁ HOLY SPIRIT CONSULT

"Let Me Sit With You in the Silence You're Afraid Of."

If the Holy Spirit could sit across from you right now, and He is, this is what He would say: "I see the weight you've been carrying. I know the moments when life felt too loud and escape felt like the only option you had. I never judged you for running to what gave you relief. I understood why it felt safer. But I want you to know you  don't have to numb yourself to survive your emotions. I can meet you in every feeling you're afraid to face."

He would continue, "Numbness seems easier because it silences the noise temporarily, but I can silence the storm permanently. I don't want to remove your emotions; I want to redeem them. I want to teach you how to hear them without being overwhelmed, how to process them without shutting down, and how to walk through them without running away. You have never been weak for escaping. You've been overwhelmed. And I am here to carry what you can't."

The Holy Spirit whispers, "I am not here to take gaming from you. I am here to take the fear out of your heart that keeps sending you to the screen. Let Me show you how to breathe again. Let Me show you how to feel without drowning. Let Me teach you the difference between peace and numbness, because you've lived so long on mute that you've forgotten how alive you can feel." He ends with this truth: ***"Bring Me the feelings you've avoided. I won't shame you. I'll heal you."***

🙏 GUIDED PRAYER

"Lord, Help Me Stop Numbing What Needs Healing."

Lord, I come to You acknowledging the truth I've been avoiding I have been using gaming and distraction to numb emotions I didn't know how to face. I confess that I've been overwhelmed, tired, and afraid of what I might feel if I slow down long enough to listen. I've called it entertainment, but deep down I know I have been using it as anesthesia.

Today, I ask for Your help. Teach me to feel again. Teach me to face my emotions with courage instead of escape. God, strengthen me in the moments when I want to run. Give me emotional clarity where I've been clouded. Give me comfort where I've been numb. Give me presence where I've been absent.

Holy Spirit, enter the places in my heart that I've muted and bring healing to the emotions I've buried. I don't want to live disconnected from myself anymore. I don't want to keep numbing pain that You are ready to transform. I surrender my escape, my overwhelm, and my avoidance. Help me step into healing, one honest moment at a time.

In Jesus 'name, amen."

REFLECTION PAGE

"What Have You Been Using Anesthesia To Avoid?"

1. **When do you use gaming as escape instead of enjoyment?**
Describe the moments, triggers, and emotional patterns.

____

____

____

____

2. **Which emotions do you feel least equipped to face without distraction?**
List them honestly, fear, sadness, anxiety, disappointment, anger.

____

____

____

____

3.   **What areas of your life have been neglected because you've been numbing instead of engaging?**
Think relationships, responsibilities, spiritual growth, or self-care.

____

____

____

____

4.   **What would healing look like if you stopped numbing and started noticing?**
Imagine your emotional life restored, not muted.

____

____

____

____

5.   **Write one truth you need to remember the next time you reach for the controller out of stress.**
Let it become your anchor.

____

____

____

____

6.   How has numbness been stolen from you?
Name the impact, lost time, lost presence, lost connections, lost clarity.

____

____

____

____

7.   What do you want God to help you feel again?
Let your heart respond.
Take your time. Feel what you've avoided. This is where healing begins.

____

____

____

____

____

____

____

____

____

____

PERSONAL NOTES

Chapter 3:

Achievement Unlocked:
Avoiding Everything That Matters

Symptom: Mastering distraction while abandoning purpose.

There's something strangely satisfying about achievements in video games. Whether it's a glowing badge, a satisfying chime, or a screen that declares your success, the rush feels immediate and rewarding. It doesn't matter how small the achievement is, "Walked Through the Door," "Jumped for the First Time," "Breathed in the General Direction of the Enemy" your brain reacts as if you just saved the world. That tiny dopamine spark tells you that you're progressing, succeeding, and accomplishing something meaningful… even if all you did was follow basic instructions or press a button at the right time.

But while you've been collecting virtual achievements like trophies in a museum, real life has been sitting in the corner, waiting for you to notice that you haven't collected much there.

In fact, if life had achievement notifications, most of yours would probably look like this: *"Achievement Failed: Returned a Text Message." "Achievement Missed: Took Care of Your Responsibilities Today." "Secret Achievement Still Locked: Showed Up Emotionally for Someone Who Needed You."* 
"Achievement Declined: Had a Hard Conversation Instead of Avoiding It."

And the worst one: "Achievement Expired: Pursued the Purpose God Gave You Before You Got Distracted."

It's not that you don't care about these things. You do. Deeply. You care about your relationships, your goals, your spiritual life, your growth, and your future. But somewhere along the way, you discovered that the discomfort of real-life responsibilities could be replaced with the immediate gratification of virtual success. Why attempt something difficult in the real world when you can feel instantly accomplished in a digital one? Why work on long-term goals when you can complete dozens of short-term quests that require no emotional risk? Why face rejection, conflict, vulnerability, growth, or failure when you can avoid all of it by leveling up in a world that demands nothing from you except time and quick thumbs?

Your avoidance isn't laziness, it's self-protection. Games offer certainty, while life offers challenge. Games offer predictable rewards, while life offers unpredictable outcomes. Games offer you a constant sense of progress, while life offers growth that is slow, invisible, and sometimes painful. It is easy to see why your brain would rather unlock a meaningless achievement than confront a meaningful responsibility. But here is the deeper truth hiding beneath avoidance: *Your soul knows you were made for more than digital progress.* Your spirit knows you were created with purpose, not just preference. Your life is longing for your presence, not your avoidance. And the calling God placed inside you is still waiting for you to stop hiding behind achievements that don't change anything.

You have mastered distraction. You've leveled up in avoidance. But the things that matter, your relationships, your growth, your mental health, your purpose, your healing, have been sitting in the background like side quests you never accepted. And every time you choose escapism over engagement, distraction over discipline, and comfort over calling, you drift further from the person you were created to become.

You don't avoid it because you're incapable. You avoid it because you're overwhelmed. You avoid it because you're afraid of failing where it matters. You avoid it because digital progress feels safer than emotional vulnerability. You avoid it because achievements in games feel easier than achievements in life. But no matter how many achievements you unlock on-screen, your heart will always feel the quiet ache of the achievements you are not unlocking, the ones tied to your destiny, your relationships, your healing, and your assignment on this earth. You were not born to live a life of avoidance. You were born to be fully alive, fully present, and fully engaged with the calling God put in you. The game gives you achievements. Life is waiting to give you purpose.

Teaching: When distraction becomes your identity and purpose becomes your casualty.

There is a reason your brain loves achievements in games, they give you the illusion of progress without requiring the vulnerability of growth. Every badge, every ding, every glowing notification tells you that you are succeeding, improving, and advancing. But what your heart never learned to distinguish is the difference between progress in a game and progress in your life. The game rewards you for your time. Life rewards you for your courage. And courage requires a level of emotional presence that avoidance tries very hard to replace.

Avoidance isn't random; it's strategic. You avoid the things that make you uncomfortable, conversations, responsibilities, expectations, conflicts, emotions, because you haven't learned how to meet discomfort without becoming overwhelmed. So, you gravitate toward environments where you feel competent. Gaming is predictable. The rules don't change. The outcomes are measurable. The rewards are instant. The characters never misinterpret you. The missions never ask for emotional honesty. The enemies don't require vulnerability. And the victories, although digital, feel real enough to trigger dopamine spikes that your brain interprets as success.

But while you've been unlocking achievements on-screen, your real life has been accumulating the opposite, uncompleted tasks, unmarked goals, unresolved emotions, unattended dreams, and unspoken truths. Life's achievements don't come with chimes or glowing badges. They require consistency, resilience, and trust. They require facing things you don't know how to face. They require stepping into the unknown instead of retreating into what feels familiar. And because life doesn't celebrate you instantly, you learned to chase the worlds that do.

Your avoidance isn't a lack of discipline; it is a lack of emotional safety. When your internal world feels unstable, uncertain, or unsupported, your mind searches for the quickest escape route. Gaming is not the problem; the purpose it took over is. It has become the place where you feel the most "successful," because it doesn't demand the parts of you that feel fragile. When reality asks for responsibility, gaming offers distraction. When reality demands growth, gaming offers comfort. When reality exposes your fears, gaming numbs them.

But here is the truth: Achievement is not the same as purpose. You can achieve endlessly in a world that doesn't require your heart, and still feel purposeless in the world that desperately needs it. You can win every level but lose yourself in the process. You can be highly skilled at defeating fictional enemies and still be avoiding the real ones, doubt, insecurity, loneliness, fear, and the calling you've been running from.

Avoiding what matters doesn't make you weak; it makes you unpracticed. You have been strengthening your ability to retreat instead of your ability to engage. You have built endurance for distraction instead of endurance for purpose. You have opened your heart to achievement while closing it to accountability. You've trained your mind to chase instant gratification and taught your soul to fear long-term meaning.

But God did not give you a life that requires a controller. He gave you a life that requires courage. Your purpose is not hidden inside a game. It is hidden inside the parts of your life you keep avoiding. The joy you want is on the other side of discomfort. The growth you crave is on the other side of showing up. The fulfillment you long for is on the other side of the things you keep pushing aside. And until you recognize that your avoidance is simply fear wearing a confident mask, you will continue to pursue achievements that impress your brain but neglect your destiny.

Chapter 3 is the turning point. The moment where you admit that your achievements in gaming have become substitutes for the achievements God designed for your life. It's not about quitting gaming. It's about quitting avoidance. You don't have to lose your hobby. You must stop losing yourself.

⚕ FAITH PRESCRIPTION

"Do One Real-Life Achievement Every Day."

Your first prescription is simple but powerful: each day, complete  one real-life achievement, not the kind that gives you trophies, but the kind that reawakens your purpose. It does not need to be grand or impressive. It can be as small as making your bed, drinking water, answering the message you avoided, opening your Bible, spending five minutes in silence, paying a bill, cleaning one corner of your room, or writing one honest thought in a journal. Your brain needs proof that progress in real life is possible, even without digital fireworks.

Your second prescription is to identify the biggest "side quest" in your life that is distracting you from your main mission. This may be overworking, sleeping excessively, scrolling endlessly, caretaking everyone except yourself, or hiding your true emotions behind humor or silence. Write it down. Naming it helps disarm it. Your third prescription is to choose one meaningful task each week that stretches you emotionally or spiritually. This could be scheduling a hard conversation, apologizing for something you've avoided addressing, starting a project you've been scared to attempt, or simply sitting with your feelings without fleeing. You don't need dramatic leaps. You need intentional, consistent engagement.

Your fourth prescription is to create an "Achievement Journal" where you record only your real-life progress. No gaming accomplishments allowed. This journal will retrain your brain to celebrate reality, not escape. Every small win counts. Every step matters. Every moment of courage deserves acknowledgment.

Your final prescription is this: **remind yourself daily that purpose grows through engagement, not avoidance.** Every time you show up, you reclaim another piece of your life.

🕊 HOLY SPIRIT CONSULT

"Your Purpose Has Not Expired Just Because You Avoided It." In the quietest moments of your avoidance, the Holy Spirit has been whispering to your soul: "You have no idea how much purpose is still inside you." While you've been busy unlocking achievements that didn't require your heart, He has been patiently guarding the ones that do. He has not scolded you for drifting. He has not punished you for avoiding. He has not withdrawn from you  because you withdrew from your calling. He has simply waited, tenderly, faithfully, consistently, for you to come back to yourself.

The Holy Spirit speaks this truth over you: "You have been hiding behind fake victories because you were afraid of failing at real ones.

But I am not calling you to be perfect. I am calling you to be present." He doesn't need you to have a five-year plan. He doesn't need you to suddenly become a hero in your own life. He simply needs you to stop running. Your purpose is not fragile. It has survived your avoidance. It has survived your numbness. It has survived your fear. The calling on your life didn't weaken just because you wandered. God is not intimidated by the time you spent escaping. He is excited about the time you're about to spend awakening.

He whispers: "Let Me turn your avoidance into awareness. Let Me turn your distraction into discipline. Let Me turn your numbness into passion. Let Me walk with you into the parts of your life you've been too afraid to approach." Your purpose hasn't vanished. It has been waiting for you to show up.

🙏 GUIDED PRAYER

"Lord, Help Me Engage With What Actually Matters."

Father, I come to You honestly. I admit that I have been chasing achievements that don't require my heart because I was afraid of the things that I do. I have avoided responsibilities, conversations, emotions, and opportunities that You have been trying to place in front of me.

I chose distraction because it felt safer than vulnerability. But today, I ask for Your strength. Help me stop hiding behind the illusion of progress. Help me stop numbing myself with achievements that never reaches my soul.

God, help me show up for my own life. Teach me how to face the things I've been avoiding with courage, wisdom, and grace. Show me how to build emotional endurance. Teach me how to be present even when presence feels uncomfortable. Heal the fear that hides beneath my avoidance. Strengthen the parts of me that feel fragile.

Remember that I do not need perfection, I need participation. I invite You into every area of my life that I have neglected. Lead me back to my purpose.

In Jesus 'name, amen."

REFLECTION PAGE

"What Have You Been Winning In Fiction But Losing In Reality?"

1. **What achievements in your life have been neglected because you've chosen virtual wins instead?**
   Reflect honestly. Name the things that matter.

____

____

____

____

2. **What emotions rise when you think about engaging with your real purpose?**
   Is it fear? Insecurity? Overwhelm? Doubt?

____

____

____

____

3. **Which real-life task have you avoided the longest? Why?**
   Write what has kept you from facing it.

---

4. **Where have you been choosing comfort over calling?**
    Identify the areas where escape feels easier than growth.

---

5. **What is one meaningful achievement you want to pursue this month?**
    Make it realistic. Make it personal.

---

6. **What does your heart feel when you imagine living with purpose instead of avoidance?**
    Describe the internal shift.

---

7. **What truth from this chapter do you want to carry with you?**

Write it down. Make it your anchor. Breathe. Reflect. Be honest. Your purpose is to call, and for the first time in a long time, you're finally listening.

PERSONAL NOTES

Chapter 4:

Your Controller Isn't Broken, Your Boundaries Are

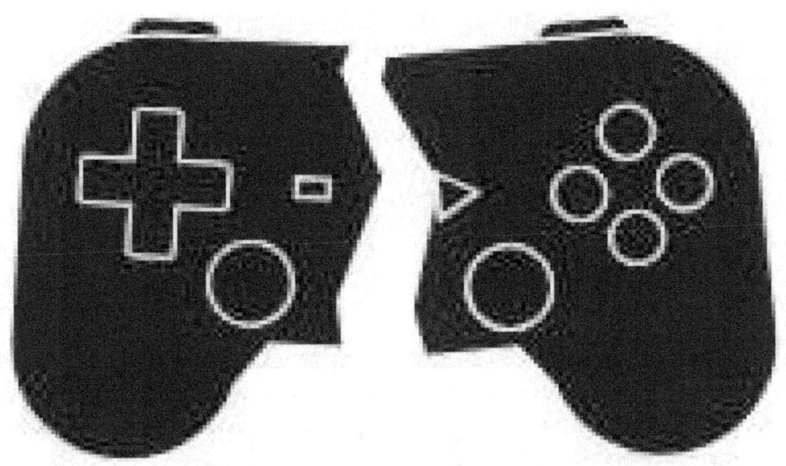

Symptom: When 'one more round 'becomes three days missing.

There's a certain kind of panic that happens when your controller stops responding, that moment when you mash every button and nothing happens. You shake it, blow on it, smack it lightly like it did something wrong, and immediately assume the controller is broken. But usually, the controller is fine. Your reaction is just dramatic because you're used to being in control. Now imagine if you react to your *actual* life the way you react to a malfunctioning controller.

Reality pauses? Emotions freeze? Responsibilities pile up. Suddenly the "controller" meaning your life, feels unresponsive, and instead of adjusting, you default to your escape: "Let me just play one round to reset my brain." But one round becomes two. Two becomes five. Five becomes three days that evaporate into digital air. And just like that, you're shocked at how far behind you are in real life, even though you can name every quest you completed, every level you beat, and every boss you defeated during your disappearance.

The symptom is simple: your controller isn't broken, your boundaries are. The issue is not your love for gaming but your lack of limits around it. Somewhere along the line, you convinced yourself that you don't need boundaries because you can "self-regulate." Except you don't. You tell yourself you'll play for 30 minutes, and then the sun sets while you're still "just finishing a mission." You promise yourself you'll handle your tasks after you game, but somehow gaming becomes the entire day, and your tasks stare at you like unpaid bills, because they are unpaid bills. You assure yourself you're in control, but the truth is that control without boundaries is just a polite form of chaos.

Boundaries are not chains; they are guardrails. They keep what you enjoy from becoming what you depend on. When your boundaries are weak, everything in your life slides out of place, your time, your priorities, your commitments, your sleep, your relationships, your emotional energy, your connection with God. Without boundaries, you're not gaming for fun anymore; you're gaming for survival. You're using time as an anesthetic instead of a resource. You're escaping instead of managing. You're disappearing instead of decompressing. You're pretending you're fine instead of admitting you're overwhelmed.

And here is the uncomfortable truth: boundaries require honesty. And honesty requires awareness. And awareness requires presence. Boundaries force you to tell yourself the truth about what you can and cannot handle emotionally. Boundaries force you to acknowledge when you're gaming because you're stressed, lonely, disappointed, or numb. Boundaries force you to admit when you're not using gaming as entertainment, you're using it as avoidance.

Your controller isn't broken. It's responding perfectly. It's you who hasn't learned how to press pause on the game long enough to press "start" on your own life.

TEACHING SECTION

"Boundaries Are Not Restrictions; They Are Your Rescue."

At some point in your life, you internalized the belief that boundaries were punishments. They meant limitation, loss, or the  removal of something that brought you comfort. But boundaries are the opposite of punishment, they are protection. They are the invisible lines that separate what strengthens you from what drains you, what is healthy from what is excessive, and what is necessary from what is destructive. Without boundaries, every good thing becomes an unhealthy thing.

Gaming without boundaries becomes escapism. Relationships without boundaries become codependency. Responsibilities without boundaries become burnout. Faith without boundaries becomes routine instead of relationship. Emotions without boundaries become chaos. Life without boundaries becomes overwhelming.

You don't struggle with gaming because the game is too powerful; you struggle because your boundaries are too weak. You struggle because your emotional self-control has eroded under the weight of stress, disappointment, and avoidance. You struggle because you haven't learned how to tell yourself "no" with compassion or "not now" with clarity.  You struggle because boundaries require discipline, and discipline requires consistency, and consistency requires emotional engagement, something you've been avoiding.

The truth is that boundaries don't restrict your freedom, they restore it. When you have boundaries, gaming becomes enjoyable again. You don't lose yourself in it; you participate in it. You don't disappear for hours; you enjoy it within limits. You don't use it to avoid emotions; you use it to unwind without losing control. Boundaries give you the freedom to play without paying the emotional price of avoidance.

The Holy Spirit is teaching you that the issue has never been the game, it's your relationship with it. You have allowed your screen to claim a role it was never designed to fill. Because when boundaries break, everything you rely on becomes a substitute for the healing you've avoided.

This chapter exists to teach you that boundaries are not just practical; they are spiritual. God uses boundaries to protect your clarity, your purpose, your mental health, and you're calling. Every time you set a boundary, heaven celebrates, because boundaries bring order, and order brings peace.

FAITH PRESCRIPTION

"Set One Boundary You Actually Keep."
Your prescription for this chapter is straightforward but transformative.

1. Set a daily gaming limit, and honor it.
Not because gaming is bad, but because your emotional health is worth more than your escape. If you choose 1 hour, honor it. If you choose 2 hours, honor it. If you choose weekends only, commit to it. Boundaries only work if you keep them.

2. Create a pre-gaming checklist.
Before you play, ask yourself:
- Did I eat?
- Did I pray?
- Did I handle my main responsibilities for the day?
- Am I playing to relax, or am I playing to disappear?

If you're using gaming to escape, pause. Do something grounding first.

3. Set a nightly cutoff.
Sleep is not optional. Your brain needs rest. Your emotions need rest. Your boundaries need rest.

4. Establish a no-gaming Sabbath.
One day a week, step away from the screen. Let your emotions reset naturally instead of electronically.

5. Have one accountability person.
Someone who knows your goals, your tendencies, and your need for boundaries. Someone who will check in with you compassionately, not criticize you. These prescriptions are not punishment. They are restoration.

HOLY SPIRIT CONSULT

"You don't need more control, you need more clarity."
If the Holy Spirit could sit with you right now, He would gently reveal this truth: "You are not weak. You are overwhelmed. And when you are overwhelmed, you reach for what feels predictable.

But I am here to help you create boundaries that give you room to breathe." He would whisper, "Your controller works fine, but your heart is tired. Let Me help you restore the boundaries you've lost. Let Me teach you how to say no without guilt and how to say yes without fear. Let Me show you that you don't need strict control, you need steady strength." The Holy Spirit is not asking you to abandon gaming. He is asking you to abandon the fear that prevents you from creating boundaries. He is inviting you to clarity, not condemnation.

GUIDED PRAYER

"Lord, Teach Me How to Protect What You're Healing."

Father, I ask You to help me rebuild the boundaries that have fallen apart in my life. I admit that I have lost control of my time, my energy, and my attention. I admit that I have used gaming to avoid reality instead of facing it. I ask You to give me wisdom to create boundaries, courage to honor them, and strength to maintain them even on difficult days.

Help me recognize when I am escaping instead of engaging. Help me choose presence over avoidance and clarity over chaos. Protect the parts of me You are healing. Strengthen the parts of me that feel fragile. And teach me how to live with balance, intention, and peace.

In Jesus 'name, amen.

REFLECTION PAGE

"Where Are My Boundaries Broken?"

1. Where in your life do you lack boundaries the most?

____

____

____

____

2. What emotions drive your need to escape?

____

____

____

____

3. Which boundaries do you avoid setting because you fear discomfort or missing out?

____

____

____

____

4. What would your life look like if your boundaries were strong?

---

5.   What boundary is God asking you to set right now?

---

6.   How can you honor that boundary today?

Let this chapter become your turning point. Your life is not out of control; your boundaries simply need rebuilding. And now, you finally have the strength to do it.

Chapter 5:

Emotional AFK: Mentally Checked Out, Spiritually Offline

Symptom: When your body is present, but your soul hits the logout button.

There's a unique kind of emptiness that happens when you're physically in the room but emotionally on another planet. You know the feeling, people talk to you, and you hear sounds but not meaning. Responsibilities appear in front of you, but your motivation is nowhere to be found. Someone asks if you're okay, and you nod because the truth feels too complicated to explain. You're not angry. You're not sad. You're not even overwhelmed. You're just… gone. It's as if your emotional hard drive crashed, and now you're stuck staring at a blinking cursor wondering if your feelings are ever going to load again. 

This is emotional AFK, being away from your own heart, even while your body pretends to function. It's when your internal system goes offline and your soul quietly steps out of the room without leaving a note. You're not avoiding life on purpose; you genuinely don't have the emotional energy to remain present. You're running on autopilot, performing tasks without processing them, responding without thinking, and existing without living. Its numbness disguised as normalcy, silence disguised as stability, burnout disguised as "I'm fine."

The symptom is not that you don't care. The symptom is that caring feels too heavy right now. Your emotions have been overstimulated for so long that your heart finally hit the emergency shut-off switch. And while your brain is trying to keep your functioning, your spirit has quietly slipped into the background, waving a tiny flag that says, "I can't keep pretending anymore."

Emotional AFK doesn't look dramatic on the outside. But on the inside, it is a slow drift away from yourself, one moment at a time.

TEACHING SECTION

"When your soul logs out, your life loses its clarity."

Emotional AFK doesn't happen overnight. It is the accumulation of stress you didn't process, feelings you didn't express, disappointments you didn't acknowledge, and responsibilities you absorbed without rest. Your emotional capacity is not infinite, it's limited, delicate, and requires care. When you don't slow down, your emotions will do it for you. When you ignore your limits, your heart will hit the brakes. When life becomes too loud, your system silently shuts down.

You didn't become emotionally offline because you're weak. You became emotionally offline because you've been trying to survive without support. You've been carrying burdens that required more strength than you had available. You've been functioning without pausing, performing without breathing, and caring for others while neglecting yourself. Emotional AFK isn't laziness; it's your heart trying to save itself from collapsing under the weight of everything you've silently endured.

But the danger of emotional AFK is that it slowly disconnects you from the very things that would heal you, relationships, vulnerability, faith, introspection, and honesty. When you go emotionally offline, you lose access to your own truth. You stop recognizing your needs. You forget what rest feels like. You lose the ability to connect with God because connection requires availability, and you haven't been emotionally available to anyone, not even yourself.

There comes a point where your heart is no longer depleted; it's depleted of the ability to even recognize depletion. That's when life feels hollow. That's when people feel far away. That's when God feels silent, not because He stopped speaking but because you're too numb to feel Him. And numbness is the quiet enemy of spiritual growth. It dulls your hunger for truth. It mutes your sensitivity to conviction. It blurs your ability to discern God's voice. It makes worship feel like noise and prayer feel like chores.

But God has compassion for emotional AFK. He doesn't shame you for shutting down; He gently calls you back. He knows that your heart is tired, your mind is stretched, and your soul is bruised. He doesn't demand that you snap out of it. He invites you to return slowly, safely, and with honesty. He teaches you that your emotional presence matters to Him, not because He needs it but because He created you to thrive, not just function. Emotional AFK is your heart's cry for restoration, and God never ignores cries for restoration.

Healing begins when you recognize two truths:

1. You are not emotionally absent because you're broken. You're emotionally absent because you're exhausted.
2. God does not expect perfection, He expects honesty.

Your soul is not malfunctioning. It is calling for maintenance.

FAITH PRESCRIPTION

"Reconnect with yourself before you try to reconnect with the world."

Your prescription for this chapter begins with gentle reconnection. No big leaps. No intense goals. No emotional marathons.

<u>1. Do one thing each day that brings your emotions back online.</u>

This could be:
- sitting in silence for five minutes
- taking a slow walk

- journaling one honest sentence
- breathing deeply
- acknowledging how you feel without minimizing i
- listening to worship music without multitasking

You don't have to feel everything at once. You just need to feel *something* again.

2. Practice emotional naming.

Whenever you feel numb, whisper: I feel disconnected right now, and that's okay. But I choose to stay present. Naming numbness reduces its power.

3. Limit your escape activities to 24 hours.

No excessive gaming, scrolling, or binge-watching. Let your emotions have room to breathe.

4. Schedule a "heart check" conversation once a week.

With God, with yourself, or with someone safe.

5. Choose one spiritual practice that brings your heart back online.

Not the ones that feel heavy, the ones that feel grounding:

- worship
- scripture meditation
- quiet prayer
- journaling
- solitude

Your prescription is not performance. It is presence.

HOLY SPIRIT CONSULT

"I know where you went, and I know how to bring you back."

If the Holy Spirit could speak to you audibly in your numbness, He would say, "I never left when you went AFK. I stayed by your side, waiting for the moment you realize you weren't abandoned; you were exhausted."

He would whisper, "I know your heart shut down because you were overwhelmed, not because you stopped caring. I know you drifted because you were tired, not because you stopped believing. I know you went quietly because you didn't have the strength to express what you were feeling. But I am not intimidated by your silence. I am not discouraged by your numbness. I know how to restore what burnout tried to steal."

The Holy Spirit is the only One who can reach you when you're emotionally offline. He doesn't demand emotional availability, He creates it. He breathes life into numb places. He brings clarity into foggy minds. He awakens hearts that have gone dormant. And He reminds you gently: **"You are still Mine, even when you feel nothing."** His presence is the invitation back on your own.

GUIDED PRAYER

"Lord, I want to come back, even if I don't know how."

God, I come before You honestly. I feel disconnected from myself, from others, and even from You. I feel numb, tired, overwhelmed, or simply absent. I admit that I have been emotionally AFK, trying to function while my soul quietly shut down. But I don't want to stay disconnected. I want to return.

Lord, help me feel again. Help me reconnect with my own heart. Help me understand the emotions I've been avoiding or unable to process. Bring my spirit back online. Awaken what has gone numb. Speak gently to the places that have grown silent. Restore my sensitivity to Your voice. Restore my clarity. Restore my presence. I surrender my numbness to You. Meet me in it. Lead me out of it. Help me to breathe again, hope again, feel again, and trust again. In Jesus 'name, amen.

REFLECTION PAGE

"Where Did I Go Emotionally, and What Will It Take to Return?"

1. **When did you start feeling emotionally AFK?**

2. **What emotions have become harder for you to access?**

3. **What stressors or disappointments drained you the most?**

4. **Which areas of your life have suffered because you've been emotionally offline?**

---

5.   **What small action can help reconnect yourself today?**

---

6.   **What do you want God to restore emotionally?**

---

7.   **What does your heart feel, even faintly, as you read this chapter?**

Be gentle with yourself. Returning emotionally is a slow walk, not a sprint. But you are returning, one honest moment at a time.

PERSONAL NOTES

Chapter 6:

Why Fictional Worlds Feel Safer Than Your Real One

Symptom: When you trust imaginary places more than the life God gave you.

There is a strange comfort in fictional worlds; the kind of comfort that makes you exhale without realizing you've been holding your breath all day. Fictional worlds are predictable. They make sense. They run on rules and patterns and logic that, even when chaotic, still feel controllable. In a fictional world, you know who the villain is, what the mission requires, and how to recover when you get knocked down. In your real life, the villains are harder to identify, the missions are unclear, the battles are emotional, and the damage doesn't disappear after loading a screen.

It is no surprise, then, that fictional worlds feel safer. They don't betray you. They don't abandon you. They don't judge you. They don't misunderstand your silence. They don't require you to articulate your pain. They don't ask you to be vulnerable. They don't change the rules without warning. And most importantly, fictional worlds do not remind you of the places in your life where trauma, disappointment, and heartbreak still breathe. The symptom is this: your mind gravitates toward fictional worlds because your real one has wounded you.

TEACHING SECTION

"Trauma taught you to escape, not to trust."

Fictional worlds didn't become safer than your real one by accident. Your nervous system was shaped by experiences where safety wasn't guaranteed, moments where people failed you, blinded you, ignored you, or didn't protect you. Trauma is not always a catastrophic event. Sometimes it is the accumulation of small heartbreaks, quiet disappointments, unmet needs, emotional neglect, chaotic environments, or seasons where you had to survive instead of live.

Trauma rewires the brain toward survival. It teaches you to scan for danger, anticipate disappointment, expect abandonment, avoid vulnerability, and retreat from anything that feels emotionally risky. When your nervous system learns "people can hurt me," it also learns "fictional places can't." And so, your brain starts retreating, not into boredom, not into entertainment, but into emotional safety. Fictional worlds become your sanctuary because they don't trigger old wounds. They don't remind you of what you lost. They don't mirror the chaos you endured. They simply offer relief. Psychologically, escape becomes a coping mechanism because it gives you something your real life didn't: control.

In fictional worlds: You control your pace. You control your failures. You control your returns. You control your narrative. You control your version of bravery. You control who you are and who you're not. Real life doesn't work like that. Real life requires surrender, not control. Real life requires vulnerability, not strategy. Real life requires emotional presence, not performance. Real life requires you to be soft in places where you once needed to be guarded.

This is why your heart retreats. Not because you hate your life, but because your life has hurt you. But here is the truth: fictional worlds may feel safer, but they offer no healing. They allow you to rest, but they cannot restore you. They let you breathe, but they cannot rebuild what broke. They quiet your mind, but they cannot mend your heart. They distract you, but they cannot deliver you. God will let you use fictional worlds for comfort, but He will never allow them to become substitutes for the wholeness He's trying to bring into your life.

Fictional worlds offer control. God offers transformation. And transformation requires you to return to the parts of your life you've been avoiding, not because they are easy, but because that is where you're healing lives.

FAITH PRESCRIPTION

"Face one real-life fear each week."

Your prescription begins with courage, the quiet kind, the kind that starts small, the kind that doesn't require perfection. Each week, you will choose one area of your real life that feels emotionally unsafe and take a tiny, strategic step toward healing it.

1. Identify one emotional trigger.
Something that makes you retreat. Something that shuts you down. Something that nudges you toward escape.

2. Do something small and safe in response.
Not overwhelming. Not dramatic.
Just one gentle action:
- Send the honest message you've been scared to send.
- Acknowledge a feeling you've ignored.
- Name the disappointment you keep avoiding.
- Admit you're hurting in one area of your life.
- Set a boundary where fear once ruled.
- Choose connection over isolation for one moment.

3. Create a "Return Plan."
Every time you feel pulled into escape, pause and ask: "What part of my real life feels unsafe right now?" Let awareness interrupt escape.

4. Limit your fictional escape time by 10%.
Not elimination, moderation. Not punishment, balance.

5. Celebrate real bravery.

Every tiny act of emotional presence is an achievement worth writing down. Healing doesn't begin when you leave fictional worlds. Healing begins when you stop running from your real one.

HOLY SPIRIT CONSULT

"I am not calling you out, I am calling you home."

If the Holy Spirit could hold your face in His hands, He would whisper to you, "I know why you feel safer in fictional worlds. I saw the moments in your life when safety was not guaranteed. I saw the nights when you cried without comfort. I saw the relationship that broke you. I saw the dreams that disappointed you. I saw the trust that was violated. I saw the version of you that Learn to survive without rest. I understand why escape became your sanctuary."

And then He would say, "But I am here to give you a different kind of safety, the kind that comes from healing, not hiding. You don't have to escape to feel safe with Me. You don't have to disappear to protect yourself. You don't have to retreat into fictional places to find peace. I can make your real life safe again."

He would continue, "The places you avoid are the places I want to restore. The wounds you hide are the ones I want to heal. The fears you bury are the ones I want to break. You don't need control to feel whole; you need My presence. And I am here, ready to walk with you back into the world you left behind."

The Holy Spirit doesn't shame your escape; He understands it. But He refuses to leave you there. Because calling lives in your real world, not your fictional one.

GUIDED PRAYER

"Lord, help me feel safe in my own life again."

Father, I come to You with honesty and vulnerability. I admit that fictional worlds have felt safer than my real one. I admit that I have been escaping because I didn't know how to face my disappointment, my trauma, my loneliness, or my fears. I admit that I have avoided emotions that felt too heavy and realities that felt too risky. But today, I ask You to help me return.

Lord, heal the parts of me that learned to survive through escape. Heal the places in my heart where fear still echoes. Heal the wounds that taught me people could not be trusted. Heal the memories that shaped my belief that safety was temporary. Bring comfort to the places where I still feel unprotected. Bring peace to the places where chaos still lingers. Bring clarity to the places where I still feel lost.

Holy Spirit shows me how to reclaim my real life with courage. Walk with me into the rooms I once avoided. Sit with me in the feelings I tried to silence. Strengthen me in the moments where escape feels easier than healing. And remind me daily that I am not walking alone, You are restoring me, one breath at a time.

In Jesus 'name, amen.

REFLECTION PAGE

"Why Does Fiction Feel Safer Than Reality?"
1. **Which fictional worlds feel like emotional safety to you? Why?**

____

____

____

____

---

2. **What parts of your real life feel unpredictable or unsafe?**

---

3. **What wound or disappointment shaped your instinct to escape?**

---

4. **What small real-world step would feel brave for you today?**

---

5.   What does God want to heal in your real life that you've been avoiding?

---

6.   Where do you need safety restored so you can stop retreating?

---

7.   What would life feel like if you trusted it again?

Take your time. This chapter is deep work. You don't heal trauma overnight, but today, you took the first step back into the world that needs your present.

Chapter 7:

You Want Control, Not Connection

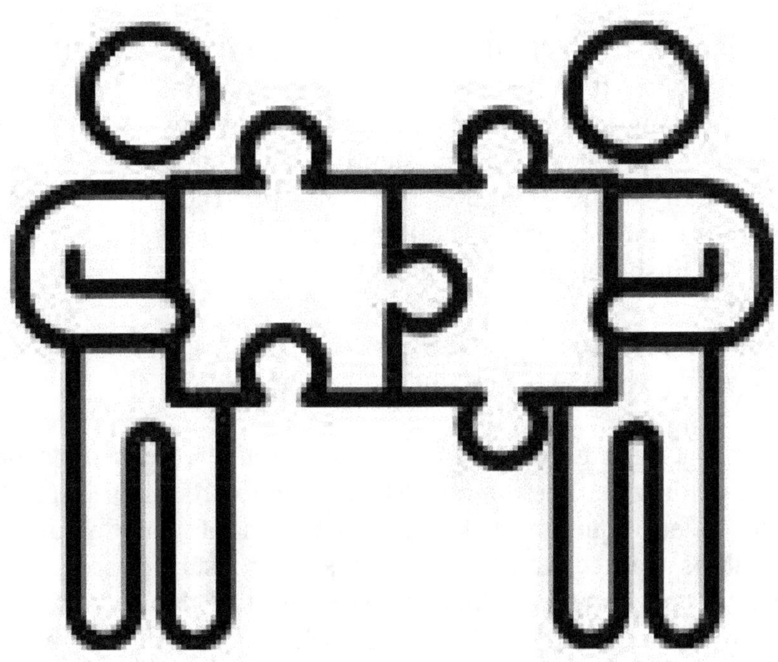

Symptom: When predictable reward systems feel safer than unpredictable people.

There's a reason you feel more confident facing a digital boss fight than facing another human being. Games, even the wildest ones, function within predictable frameworks. If you do X, you get Y. If you follow a pattern, you get a reward. If you mess up, the consequence is clear and contained. No confusion. No emotional whiplash. No unexpected reactions. No stab wounds from someone's tone, someone's silence, or someone's inability to love you the way you hoped.

People, on the other hand, are unpredictable. They change. They misunderstand. They are disappointed. They withdrew. They say they're fine when they're clearly not. They apologize without meaning it or mean it without knowing how to change. They love inconsistently. They hurt unintentionally. They require patience, presence, vulnerability, and compromise, all things that feel far riskier than pushing buttons on a controller.

And so, the symptom becomes clear: You prefer the control of digital worlds over the uncertainty of human ones.

You're not avoiding connection because you're cold or detached. You're avoiding connection because connection requires surrender, and surrender requires trust. But trust is hard when your past relationships trained your nervous system to stay guarded, stay hidden, or stay quiet. Control feels easier than connection. Predictability feels safer than vulnerability. Reward systems feel easier to understand than human emotions. And so, without realizing it, you've slowly shaped your life around environments where *you* determine the outcome, where nothing surprises you, nothing blinds you, nothing demands too much of you, and nothing has the power

96

to hurt you. But what also happens quietly is that nothing has the power to love you deeply either.

TEACHING SECTION

"Predictability feels like peace when your history is full of chaos."

The human brain craves patterns, consistency, and predictability, especially if your emotional history includes disappointment, rejection, or chaos. When real-life relationships feel unstable, your nervous system retreats to environments that offer certainty.

Gaming rewards the exact behaviors your heart learned to value:

✓ Consistency
✓ Control
✓ Predictable outcomes
✓ Clear goals
✓ Immediate feedback
✓ Fairness (even in chaos)
✓ Achievement without vulnerability

These things make your brain feel safe because they don't activate your emotional wounds. You don't have to wonder if the game is mad at you. You don't have to decode its tone. You don't have to feel guilty about needing space. You don't have to risk disappointing it. You don't have to question your worth. You don't have to be "too much" or "not enough." You simply show up and do what the system expects, and the system rewards you.

But people?
People don't work like that.
People are in moods.
People have histories.

People have needs.
People have wounds. People have breaking points.
People have inconsistencies.
People have trauma responses.
People have emotional storms.
People have invisible expectations.

People have lawyers and they don't know how to communicate. Connecting with real humans requires emotional flexibility, not just predictable effort. It requires empathy, discernment, and patience. It requires sitting in silence, navigating tension, asking hard questions, and embracing uncomfortable truths. Most importantly, it requires surrender, letting parts of yourself be seen, known, and vulnerable without the guarantee of a perfect response.

Control feels safer than surrender. And surrender scares people  whose trust has been mishandled. This is why you run toward environments where *you* hold the power and away from environments where you could get wounded. But here is the truth: **Control is not the same as peace.**

Control is avoidance wearing the clothes of stability. Control is safety built on fear, not freedom. Control is comfort built on isolation. Control is predictability built on the absence of real intimacy. Connection requires risk, but it also offers the emotional depth that your soul is starving for. You don't want isolation. You want safety. You don't want control. You want consistency. You don't want distance. You want reassurance. You don't want detachment. You want a love that won't shift beneath your feet.

But healing will require you to do something brave: Step out of controlled spaces and into relational ones, slowly, safely, and with support. You don't need to jump into deep relationships. You just need to stop hiding behind controlled ones.

FAITH PRESCRIPTION

"Practice connection in small, low-risk ways."
Your prescription is not to force intimacy or push yourself into overwhelming conversation. The goal is not speeding, it's strength.

1) *Practice connection in safe, tiny doses.*
Say hello to someone instead of avoiding eye contact. Respond to a text instead of ghosting. Say "thank you" sincerely. Ask someone how they're doing and listen. You don't need depth, you need engagement.

2) *Identify where control is hiding.*
Write down the places in your life where you choose predictability over connection:
- friendships
- family
- church
- dating
- conversations
- vulnerability

Naming control exposes fear.

3) *Invite one safe person into one honest moment each week.*
Not your whole story, just one emotion. One truth. One struggle.
One need. You're not trying to "connect perfectly."
You're trying to give connection permission.

4) *Reduce one control habit.*
This could be:
- overplanning
- emotional shutdown
- withdrawing when uncomfortable

- avoiding relational conversations
- micromanaging your schedule

Replace control with curiosity.

5) *Pray daily for courage to be emotionally present.*
You don't need to be soft everywhere, just open enough to not feel alone inside yourself.

HOLY SPIRIT CONSULT

"You learned control for survival, but I can teach you connection for healing."

If the Holy Spirit could sit with you in your cautious, guarded, self-protected heart, He would say, "I know why you chose control. I saw the moments when connection hurt more than loneliness. I saw the relationship that disappointed you. I saw the ways people mishandled your trust. I saw the seasons where vulnerability cost you more than it rewarded you."

And then He would whisper with tenderness, "But I have not called you to a life where you need to protect yourself from love. I have called you to relationships that are safe, healing, and grounded in grace. You don't have to be strong everywhere. You don't have to be perfect. You don't have to control the outcome. You just need to let Me show you how to connect without losing yourself."

He continues, "I will teach you how to love without fear, how to trust without panic, how to rest without retreating, and how to show up without shutting down. You don't need to control everything when you trust Me with the things you can't."

The Holy Spirit is not asking you to surrender to people, He is asking you to surrender the fear that keeps you from them.

GUIDED PRAYER

"Lord, help me release control and open my heart again."
God, I confess that I have been choosing control over connection because control feels safer. I have used predictability to protect myself from disappointment, rejection, and emotional chaos. I admit that I have pulled away from people, not because I don't care, but because I don't feel safe. But I don't want to live guarded anymore. I want to live connected.

Lord, help me lower my walls without losing my wisdom. Help me trust again, slowly, safely, and with Your guidance. Heal the fears that taught me to retreat. Heal the wounds that made control feel necessary. Heal the disappointment that made connections feel dangerous. Open my heart to the right people, the right community, and the right relationships. Lead me toward connection that reflects Your love. In Jesus 'name, amen.

REFLECTION PAGE

"Where Is Control Replacing Connection in My Life?"
1. **What relationship or memory taught you that people weren't safe?**

____

____

____

____

2. ***Where do you seek predictability because connection feels risky?***

____

____

____

____

3.   What would happen if you let someone see one honest
     emotion today?

____

____

____

____

4.   Where is God inviting you to surrender control gently?

____

____

____

____

5.   What connection in your life feels spiritually healthy,
     even if it feels scary?

____

____

____

____

6.   How would your life change if you trusted more and controlled less?

____

____

____

____

____

7.   What truth from this chapter do you want to carry forward?

____

____

____

____

____

____

____

____

____

Connection is not built in one day, but it begins with one courageous moment of presence.

PERSONAL NOTES

Chapter 8:

Comfort Over Calling, When God Has To Compete With A Console

Symptom: When your purpose becomes optional, but gaming never does.

There's a moment you rarely admit out loud, the moment you realize you have more consistency with your console than with your calling. You never forget raid night, but somehow you forgot the dream you prayed for two years ago. You can grind for digital loot for hours, but the moment God asks you for ten minutes of quiet, your spirit suddenly develops "attention span arthritis." You never seem to miss an update on your favorite game, but missing devotion time? That somehow feels justified, excusable, or "God understands." The truth is painfully simple: you haven't stopped loving God; you've just grown comfortable loving other things more consistently than Him.

The symptom is not rebellion. It's drift, slow, subtle, silent drift. You didn't wake up one day and choose passivity. You slide into it gradually, the way someone slips into warm water without noticing how deep they've gone. Spiritual drift is never loud; it's quiet and polite. It shows up as "I'll pray later," "I'm too tired," or "Let me finish this round," until suddenly *later* becomes never, *tired* becomes your personality, and *this round* has stretched into hours you can't account for. Comfort becomes your refuge while calling becomes your inconvenience.

You're not spiritually dead; you're spiritually dormant. Your gifts didn't disappear; they went numb from lack of use. Your passion didn't die; it just got overshadowed by the easy, predictable dopamine hits of digital worlds. And God hasn't stopped speaking; you've just grown comfortable ignoring the quiet parts of your soul that used to respond to Him eagerly. Comfort didn't steal your call; it slowly replaced it with something easier.

TEACHING SECTION

The Slow Drift From Purpose to Passivity

Passivity never announces itself. It sneaks in through postponed prayers, watered-down discipline, and emotional exhaustion disguised as "I just need a break." Purpose requires pursuit; comfort requires nothing. And because comfort demands nothing from you, it becomes the easiest place to hide when life feels overwhelming or unpredictable. You didn't abandon your call; you simply stopped chasing it with the urgency it deserves.

The slow drift starts with small compromises. You stop checking in with God regularly. You pray on the go instead of with intention. Your silence convictions that once stirred you. You lose urgency for the things that once burned in your heart. You become too fatigued for spiritual pursuits but always energized for escapism. The shift is so subtle that you don't recognize what's happening until you wake up one day and realize your purpose hasn't moved, *you* have. Purpose is stationary; calling is steady; assignment is constant, but passivity makes you drift away from all three as if you are floating on lazy water believing the current isn't strong enough to take you anywhere dangerous.

The psychology behind this drift is simple: the brain gravitates toward environments where it feels competent, rewarded, and unchallenged. Games provide that instantly. Purpose does not. Purpose stretches you. It exposes insecurities. It requires long-term endurance. It asks you to confront fear, step outside your comfort zone, engage with people, develop discipline, and trust God without a walkthrough guide. Purpose makes you face yourself. Comfort lets you avoid yourself. And so, without realizing it, you consistently choose the world where you feel powerful over the world where you must learn to grow.

But spiritually, the drift is deeper than psychology, it's a heart posture slowly shifting from hunger to complacency. When your spirit stops craving God's presence, something else will fill the silence. When your heart stops leaning into purpose, entertainment will become your emotional crutch. When you stop showing up for your call, your comfort will gladly take its place.

God is not competing with your console because He's insecure. He's competing because He knows comfort creates counterfeit fulfillment. Comfort feels like peace, but it's sedation. Comfort feels like rest, but it's stagnating. Comfort feels like relief, but its avoidance wearing the disguise of "I deserve this." Comfort numbs spiritual hunger until you don't realize how malnourished your calling has become. You become spiritually "full" of things that have no nutritional value.

The slow drift from purpose to passivity happens when you prioritize ease over encounter, distraction over discipline, and relief over responsibility. But the calling of God on your life is not fragile, it didn't vanish just because you drifted. It's still there, intact, vibrant, waiting, patient. God has not withdrawn it. You haven't lost it. You have simply stopped moving toward it.

The good news? Drift is reversible. One decision can break spiritual passivity. One moment of honesty can reignite hunger. One step toward God can revive calling. One conversation with Him can re-center your spirit. Purpose doesn't require perfection. It requires *presence*. Calling doesn't require certainty. It requires *surrender*. Destiny doesn't require nonstop hustle. It requires *alignment*.

You don't need to feel ready to return. You just need to stop choosing comfort over the God who created you for more. And when do you do it? Your calling will meecallalf way.

"Rebuild Your Rhythm, One Small Yes at a Time."
Your prescription for this chapter is not intensity, it's consistency. God isn't asking for dramatic leaps. He's asking for small, faithful steps that shift your heart from comfort back toward calling. You will rebuild your spiritual momentum one yes at a time.

1. Choose a daily spiritual practice you can commit to.
Not the "I will pray three hours a day and memorize Leviticus" version you promise when you're emotionally hyped, the sustainable version:
- one scripture a day
- one honest prayer
- a five-minute worship moment
- a single journal sentence
- a quiet pause before bed
-

Your call doesn't need a marathon. It needs a heartbeat.

2. Set a daily "God-first moment."
Not morning, not night, just the *first moment* when you remember Him. Before you scroll. Before you play. Before you escape. A moment of alignment brings your purpose back into focus.

3. Limit comfort-driven escape.
Not elimination, reduction. If you play for three hours, try two. If you escape daily, try giving God one of those days. If you avoid responsibility, finish one task before you rest. Comfort becomes toxic when it consumes the time meant for calling.

4. Do one assignment each week tied to your purpose.

Just *one*. Something that stirs the part of you God awakened. Your gift is not dead, it's under-stimulated. Revive it gently.

5. Ask God for hunger.

When you stop feeling spiritually hungry, that's not failure, it's a sign you've been feeding yourself with the wrong things. Pray this daily: Lord, increase my hunger for You again. Your prescription is simple:

Move toward God in small ways, He will meet you in big ones.

HOLY SPIRIT CONSULT

"I refuse to let comfort steal what you were created to carry."

If the Holy Spirit could sit across from you right now, and He is, He would speak to you with both tenderness and authority: *"I know why you've drifted. I know the weight you carry, the fatigue beneath your surface, the pressure you don't talk about, and the disappointments you pretend don't matter. I know comfort feels safer than purpose because comfort doesn't ask anything from you. But hear Me clearly: your comfort cannot give you what only your calling can."* He continues, You think your passion died, but it didn't. It's just buried under fatigue, fear, and distraction. I have been guarding it until you are ready to return. I am not calling you back to strive; I am calling you back to alignment. You don't need to force purpose; you simply need to stop running from it."

Then He whispers, You were created for more than numbing your days away. You were created to carry something eternal, something powerful, something heaven placed inside you long before entertainment began competing for your attention. I am not angry that you drifted, but I will not let you stay asleep. I am stirring the part of you that comfort silenced. I am awakening the part of you that destiny still needs."

And finally, with gentleness: "Come back to Me. Come back to what lights your soul on fire. Come back to life that requires your presence, not your avoidance. I will walk with you. I will steady you. I will strengthen you. You do not have to return alone."

🙏 GUIDED PRAYER

"Lord, pull me out of comfort and back into calling."

Father, I come before You acknowledge something I've been afraid to admit I have chosen comfort over calling. I have drifted, not because I stopped loving You, but because I grew tired, overwhelmed, disappointed, and distracted. I allowed comfort to replace obedience. I allowed entertainment to numb what You were trying to awaken. I allowed passivity to silence the purpose You placed inside of me.

Lord, thank You for not abandoning me in my drift. Thank You for loving me through my distractions. Thank You for still wanting to use me even when I stopped showing up. Today, I ask for Your help. Pull me out of the places where comfort trapped me. Stir my spirit again. Reignite my hunger. Restore my passion. Renew my clarity. Remind me of the assignment I walked away from. Strengthen me to choose presence over passivity.

Holy Spirit, break the chains of comfort that have quietly held me back. Give me the courage to pursue what You designed me to do. Give me the discipline to rebuild my spiritual rhythm. Give me the desire to return to the things that once set my soul on fire. Help me follow You with fresh conviction and renewed obedience. In Jesus 'name, amen.

REFLECTION PAGE

"Where Did Comfort Replace My Calling?"

Use this reflection section to bring clarity to the drift you've been experiencing, NOT to shame yourself, but to awaken yourself.

1. **Where has comfort become easier than obedience in your life?**

____

____

____

____

2. **What calling, gift, or purpose did you quietly set aside when life got overwhelming?**

____

____

____

____

3. **What emotions pull you into passivity most often (fear, exhaustion, disappointment, insecurity)?**

____

____

____

____

4. **What part of your spiritual routine drifted first? Why?**

____

____

____

____

5.   What assignments from God do you still feel in your spirit, even if you haven't acted on them?

____

____

____

6.   What small step can you take this week to move toward your calling again?

____

____

____

7.   Where do you need supernatural strength, not personal willpower?

____

____

____

Write honestly. Listen deeply. Let God reawaken what comfort tried to silence. Your calling didn't die; it's waiting for your return.

PERSONAL NOTES

Chapter 9:

You're Not Tired, You're Soul-Exhausted

Symptom: When emotional depletion masquerades as ordinary fatigue.

There is a kind of exhaustion that sleep can't fix, the kind that makes you wake up just as drained as when you go to bed. It is not physical. It is not simply mental. It is deeper, heavier, and more suffocating. It's exhaustion that comes from carrying unspoken emotions, unresolved stress, and unhealed wounds for far too long. It's when you've been functioning on empty, pretending you're fine, and holding your breath emotionally without ever exhaling.

This exhaustion doesn't show up as yawning or droopy eyes, it shows up as numbness, avoidance, irritability, escapism, and the quiet longing to disappear into anything that doesn't demand your heart's attention.

You think you're tired, but what you really are is *emotionally bankrupt*. You think you need rest, but what you need is *renewal*. You think you're drained from activity, but you're really drained from feeling alone in what you carry. You think you're fatigued, but your soul is whispering, "I can't keep holding this."

Soul-exhaustion makes simple tasks feel overwhelming. It makes conversations feel like mountains. It makes decisions feel like battles. It makes emotions feel too loud, too heavy, too much. And so, you retreat into easier worlds, digital ones, where you don't have to show up fully.

Where you don't have to think. Where you don't have to feel. Where you don't have to confront anything inside of you that feels like too much. This is not laziness. This is not a lack of discipline. This is not "being dramatic. This is emotional depletion, the kind that turns escapism into survival.

TEACHING SECTION

"Emotional depletion fuels escapist cycles, not because you're weak, but because you're empty."
Soul-exhaustion is different from physical tiredness. Physical tiredness is fixed by a nap. Emotional depletion is fixed by emotional honesty. When you avoid or suppress what you feel, your emotions don't disappear, they hide, and they drain you slowly from the inside. Think of it like running a device with ten apps open in the background: nothing looks wrong, but everything is draining the battery. You are not malfunctioning, you are overloaded.

The psychology behind escapist cycles is clear: when your emotional system is depleted, your brain searches desperately for relief. It wants anything that quiets the noise and lifts the weight. Gaming offers instant escape. It gives your heart a false sense of rest without requiring the vulnerability that real healing demands. The problem is not the game, it is the soul-level exhaustion that makes the game feel like the only place you can breathe. 

Human beings cannot function without emotional processing. Every unprocessed feeling becomes emotional clutter. Every disappointment you avoid becomes emotional weight. Every heartbreak you suppress becomes emotional exhaustion. Every fear you ignore drains your strength. When your heart is full of unresolved emotion, everything in your life requires more energy, relationships, responsibilities, conversations, spiritual practices, even joy itself.

Soul exhaustion is what happens when you've been showing up for everyone except yourself. When you've been running on emotional fumes. When you haven't had a safe place to rest, express, cry, or release. When you've been pretending, you're okay because the world around you doesn't slow down long enough for you to admit you're not.

Here is the spiritual truth: Your soul needs what escapism cannot give you, restoration, not relief. Escapism numbs you. Restoration heals you. Escapism postpones your pain. Restoration processes it. Escapism empties you further. Restoration fills you again.

God never designed your soul to carry everything alone. Spiritual exhaustion is the result of emotional isolation. When you drift from God emotionally, you drift from the source of renewal. When you stop bringing your heart to Him, your soul begins to suffocate under the weight of what you were never meant to carry.

But here is the hopeful part: soul-exhaustion is not a sign of failure. It is a sign that something deep inside you is ready for healing. It is a sign that your soul is craving rest, not sleep, release, not entertainment, presence, not distraction, refuge, not retreat. God does not condemn your exhaustion; He calls you to come home and breathe again.

💊 FAITH PRESCRIPTION

"Rest your soul, not just your body."

Your prescription for this chapter focuses on restoration, not productivity, not performance, and religious pressure. Just restoration.

1. Schedule a daily "soul reset moment."
Five minutes. Breathe. Sit with yourself. Acknowledge one emotion, no matter how small. Your soul heals through awareness, not avoidance.

2. Choose one emotion to process each day.

Ask yourself: What am I carrying that I haven't admitted? Write it. Say it. Confess it to God. Light reduces emotional weight.

3. Replace one escape activity with one connecting activity.

Gaming is fine, but balance it with grounding practices:

- journaling
- prayer
- a walk
- worship
- talking to someone safe
- silence

You don't heal in escape. You heal in connection.

4. Do one act of compassion toward your own heart daily.

Rest without guilt. Say "no" to something draining. Hydrate. Breathe. Cry if you need to. Your soul needs softness.

5. End each day with one closing prayer: Lord, I release what drained me today. Your soul will breathe again.

🕊 HOLY SPIRIT CONSULT

"Bring Me your exhaustion, I know how to refill what life emptied."

If the Holy Spirit could sit beside you right now, He would place His hand on your chest, not to judge you, but to calm you. He would say, "I know the weight you carry. I see the exhaustion behind your smile. I see the fight in your eyes. I see the strength you've been using to hold yourself together. I see the emotional heaviness you've been afraid to acknowledge."

He would whisper, "You are not tired, you are overwhelmed. You are not weak, you are worn. You are not lazy, you are depleted. You have been running without rest, pouring without refilling, showing up without support. I am not here to criticize your exhaustion. I am here to restore your soul." He continues, "Let Me refill the places that feel empty. Let Me restore what disappointment drained. Let Me lift the burdens you were never supposed to carry alone. Let Me breathe peace into the corners of your heart where anxiety has lived too long." The Holy Spirit doesn't just see your exhaustion; He knows how to heal it.

🙏 GUIDED PRAYER

"Lord, restore my soul where life has emptied me."

Father, I come to You exhausted, not just physically, but emotionally and spiritually. I admit that I have been carrying more than I can handle alone. I confess that I have used escape to cope with the weight of my life. But today, I chose honesty. I choose openness. I choose to let You into the places I've been hiding.

Lord, restore what life drained out of me. Heal the parts of me that are tired from unspoken pain. Strengthen the parts of me that have been running on empty. Fill the places in me that feel hollow, numb, or overwhelmed. Help me return to myself. Help me return to You. Help me breathe again.

I surrender my exhaustion to You. Meet me in it. Lift the weight. Renew my strength. Rebuild my peace. Restore my soul. In Jesus ' name, amen.

REFLECTION PAGE

"What Is Draining My Soul?"
1.   **What emotional weight have you been carrying silently?**

2.   Which responsibilities drain you the fastest? Why?

3.   Where do you feel the most depleted in your life?

4.   What emotions have you been suppressing instead of processing?

5.   What would soul-rest look like for you this week?

____

____

____

____

6.   Where do you need God's renewal the most?

____

____

____

____

7.   What truth from this chapter brought clarity to your
     exhaustion?

____

____

____

____

____

Your exhaustion is not the end; it is the beginning of your
restoration.

Chapter 10:

Face The Boss Battle You've Been Avoiding: Your Life

Symptom: When every confrontation feels easier in a game than in your real world.

There is silent honesty gamers rarely admit you can face a fifty-foot digital monster without blinking, but one uncomfortable real-life conversation feels like the end of the world. You can strategize, grind, and level up for hours, but the moment God invites you to confront a financial mess, a relationship issue, a spiritual drift, a personal wound, or an overdue responsibility, suddenly your courage evaporates. Your spirit tightens. Your anxiety spikes. You  feel small again, not because you're incapable, but because your real-life battles don't come with clear instructions, predictable attacks, or a respawn button.

This symptom is simple: you can defeat fictional enemies because they don't require emotional vulnerability. In a game, the enemy is obvious. The path is predictable. The goal is structured. The consequences are limited. But your real-life boss's battles require honesty, accountability, discipline, emotional presence, boundaries, forgiveness, spiritual courage, and the willingness to stand in places where you once felt powerless. Real life doesn't let you choose your difficulty setting. It doesn't color-code the threats. It doesn't pause when you panic. It doesn't let you save your progress before you take a risk. It demands the version of you who shows up.

The truth is not that your life is too big, it's that your fear is unprocessed. The truth is not that your battles are impossible, it's that you've never learned how to confront them without escape. The truth is not that you're weak, it's that you keep running from the places where your strength is built. You're not avoiding life because you're lazy. You're avoiding life because your unresolved pain still intimidates you. And escapism has convinced your nervous system that fictional courage is easier than real courage.

TEACHING

"The boss battle isn't the problem, the fear of feeling is."

Every major "boss battle" in your life has one thing in common: emotional risk. That's the part your heart keeps dodging. You can fight dragons all day, but fight your own procrastination? Facing your debt? Confronting your loneliness? Addressing family dysfunction? Healing childhood trauma? Acknowledging addiction patterns? Ending toxic cycles? Returning to the calling you abandoned?

Those aren't just battles, they are emotional summons. And emotional summons requires something that gaming doesn't strengthen **vulnerability.** The reason you avoid battles in your own life is not because they're too difficult, it's because they're too exposed. Digital battles don't require you to feel anything. Real-life battles require you to *feel everything you've been avoiding*. Anger. Shame. Grief. Confusion. Fear. Loss. Responsibility. Discomfort. Truth.

Games reward your skill. Life confronts your soul. Games reward repetition. Life demands transformation. Games reward strategy. Life requires surrender. Games reward progress. Life reveals character. Escapism teaches you to cope, but calling teaches you to confront. And you cannot conquer what you keep avoiding.

The slow drift into avoidance begins when life grows heavy, your emotions grow loud, and you no longer trust yourself to handle what overwhelms you. So, you retreat into worlds where the only thing required is focus, not vulnerability. Where you can feel strong without being exposed. Where you can feel competent without risking disappointment. Where you can feel purposeless without confronting pain. But the escape becomes a trap: the more you avoid your life, the bigger your battles grow.

The truth is this: the real boss's battle is not your circumstances; it is your avoidance. Avoidance drains your confidence. Avoidance shrinks your identity. Avoidance increases your fear. Avoidance delays your healing. Avoidance multiplies your problems. Avoidance always creates the illusion that "later" is safer. But later becomes never and never becomes bondage. Life is not asking you to be fearless, life is asking you to be honest. God is not asking you to feel ready, He is asking you to stop running.

Healing is not asking you to confront everything at once, it's asking you to confront one thing at a time with humility, courage, and faith. And here is the truth your soul keeps whispering beneath your fear: **You can defeat digital bosses because you already carry the strength to defeat real ones, you just need to redirect your courage.**

FAITH PRESCRIPTION

"Confront one thing you've been avoiding, today."
Your prescription is simple but spiritually potent.

1. Identify your real-life boss's battle.
Not all of them, just one:
- A financial pattern
- A relationship wound
- A conversation you're scared to have
- A responsibility you've been dodging
- A spiritual assignment you've paused
- A habit that keeps you stuck

Name it. Clarity breaks avoidance.

2. Break the battle into small, doable tasks.
Your brain fears big things. Break big into small. Small into tiny. Tiny into "I can do that today."

3. Give yourself a 10-minute action window.
Not an hour. Not a day. Ten minutes of courage dismantles months of avoidance.

4. Replace escape with honesty, once a day.
When you feel the pull to run, stop and ask: What am I scared to confront right now? Then breathe. Acknowledge it. And take one step toward it.

5. End each day with this prayer
"Lord, give me courage to face the life You gave me." Your life is not the enemy, fear is. And fear loses its power the moment you stop running.

✂ HOLY SPIRIT CONSULT

"I will not let fear define your future, stand and face what I've already equipped you for."

If the Holy Spirit could stand beside you before your biggest life battle, He would not scold you; He would steady you. He would whisper, "You're not stepping into this alone. I am here. I am with you. I am in you. I am strengthening you in ways you cannot yet see." He would say, I know what you've been avoiding. I know the memories that frighten you. I know the conversations that make your hands shake. I know the responsibilities that overwhelm you. I know the wounds that still ache. But I also know the strength I placed inside you, strength you haven't tapped into because fear convinced you that you were unprepared.

Then He would declare, You are more equipped than you feel. I have already gone ahead of you. I have already softened hearts, opened doors, aligned timing, and made a way. All I need is your courage, not perfection, not performance, just courage. And lovingly He would add, The battle you're avoiding is the battle that will break the chains you've carried for years. Stop running. Turn around. Stand firm. I will fight with you."

🙏 GUIDED PRAYER

"Lord, give me the courage to face what I've been escaping."

God, I come to You humbly and honestly. I admit that I've been avoiding the battles in my own life because fear felt louder than faith. I confess that escapism has been easier than confrontation. I've run from responsibilities, emotions, healing, and truth, not because I don't care, but because I've been overwhelmed and afraid.

Today, I ask for courage. Courage to stop running. Courage to confront what scares me. Courage to trust You in the places where I feel weak. I hope to show up for my own life again.

Lord, lead me into boldness. Help me break avoidance. Help me face what I've delayed. Help me feel what I've numbed. Help me walk into the battles that will build the person You've called me to be. You are my strength. You are my shield. You are my companion in every battle. I will not fight alone. In Jesus 'name, amen.

REFLECTION PAGE

"What Have I Been Avoiding, and Why?"
1. **What is the one life-battle you've been avoiding the longest? Why?**

2.   **What emotions rise when you think about confronting it?**

3.   **How has avoidance affected your peace, purpose, or relationships?**

4.   **What would change if you took one small step toward this battle today?**

____

____

5. **Where do you sense God giving you strength right now? What lie is afraid been telling you about this battle?**

____

____

____

____

6. **What truth from this chapter gives you courage to move forward?**

____

____

____

____

____

____

____

Write boldly. Reflect honestly. Your life is not meant to be escaped, it's meant to be lived, conquered, and redeemed.

Chapter 11:

Unplugging Without Falling Apart

Symptom: When disconnecting from your escapes feels like losing your stability.

Unplugging sounds easy until you try it. You tell yourself, "I'll just take a break," but the moment you step away from the game, your chest tightens, your mind searches for distraction, and your emotions the ones you've been avoiding, begin knocking on the door you hoped would stay shut. You don't fall apart because you're weak. You fall apart because your escape has become a coping mechanism that keeps your inner world quiet, controlled, and manageable. When you unplug, you're not just stepping away from entertainment, you're stepping into everything you've been suppressing.

The symptom is this: you don't fear being offline, you fear being present. Being plugged in keeps your mind occupied. Being unplugged leaves room for thoughts you don't want to think, feelings you don't want to feel, and memories you don't want to revisit. Gaming isn't an addiction, *emotional avoidance* is. You're

not terrified of silence; you're terrified of what silence might reveal. You're not afraid of boredom; you're afraid of truth. You're not afraid of stepping away from the screen; you're afraid you won't know how to stand on your own without it.

You've built stability around systems that require no emotional risk. Unplugging feels like ripping the safety net you've relied on. And so the moment you try to step away, your nervous system panics, not because the game is your lifeline, but because you haven't built emotional stamina in your real one.

TEACHING SECTION

"**Boundaries and moderation aren't punishments, they're protection.**"

Unplugging doesn't hurt because the console is powerful, it hurts because your coping system is fragile. When your emotional world goes unaddressed, your life begins to rely on the predictable comfort of digital immersion. That immersion feels safe because it does not judge, overwhelm, or expose you. It controls stimulation, something you can predict, manage, and exit at will. Real life doesn't offer that luxury. Real life has unpredictability, emotional demand, and relational complexity. Escapism offers order. Life offers growth. And growth is uncomfortable.

When you unplug, your emotional system wakes up like a limb that has been asleep, tingling, uncomfortable, stiff, and overwhelmed. You convince yourself something is wrong with you, when something is waking up in you. Moderation feels like withdrawal only because you haven't built emotional stamina. Stamina comes from learning to sit with your feelings, not run from them. It comes from allowing yourself to feel discomfort without panicking. It comes from realizing your emotions will not kill you, they're simply informing you. Boundaries with gaming aren't about restriction; they're about restoration. Moderation isn't about punishment; it's about balance. Unplugging isn't about losing pleasure; it's about reclaiming presence.

The reason you fall apart when you unplug is because your emotional world has been left unexercised. You can be socially strong, spiritually gifted, and mentally sharp, but emotionally unconditioned. Emotional stamina is built the same way physical stamina is through consistent exposure to discomfort in safe, controlled, and intentional ways. That's why moderation matters. It forces your emotional muscles to function instead of shutting down. Spiritual wisdom plays a role here too: when you're always plugged into distraction, you're rarely plugged into God. When your soul is constantly receiving stimulation, it never receives stillness. When your mind is always occupied, it never listens. Boundaries create breathing room, room for clarity, room for healing, room for conviction, room for prayer, room for self-awareness.

And here are the truth people rarely admit: You don't need entertainment removed; you need your soul strengthened. Your life will not fall apart without a console. But your emotional system might tremble while it learns how to stand on its own again. And that trembling is not failure, it is recovery.

💊 FAITH PRESCRIPTION

"Moderation is the medicine, consistency is the cure."

Your prescription for this chapter is not detox, it is discipline.
1. Set structured play windows.
Choose specific times to play instead of using gaming as background emotional noise. Predictability builds emotional stability.

2. Practice daily unplug moments.
Five minutes of pure silence. No screens. No stimulation. No escape. Just presence. Your soul needs that clarity.

3. Build emotional stamina slowly.
Sit with a feeling for 60 seconds before escaping. Then 2 minutes. Then 5. This is emotional conditioning; it will save your life.

4. Replace one escape session with one connection session per week.
Call someone. Pray. Go outside. Journal. Let your heart interact with the real world.

5. Set a "no gaming after this time" boundary.
Your brain needs nightly detoxes to reset emotionally and spiritually.

6. Practice emotional honesty daily.

Every night ask yourself: What emotion did I avoid today?" Write it. Acknowledge it. Add no shame. Moderation won't make you less happy; it will make you more whole.

✥ HOLY SPIRIT CONSULT

"You won't fall apart, I'm teaching you how to stand."

If the Holy Spirit could speak directly into your moment of panic when you unplug, He would whisper, "You're not losing yourself, you're finding yourself." He would say, "I know unplugging feels like you're pulling away from safety. But the safety you built was temporary, and I'm teaching you how to build something permanent, emotional strength, spiritual clarity, and inner peace."

He would continue, "You are not fragile. You are not dependent. You are not weak. You are simply healing. And healing makes your emotions loud before it makes your heart quiet. Do not fear the noise, I am in the noise. Do not fear the silence, I am in the silence. Do not fear the stillness, I am in the stillness."

Then He would add with tenderness, The world you escape into is predictable, but the presence you avoid is powerful. I am not asking you to disconnect from joy, I am asking you to disconnect from avoidance. You won't fall apart when you unplug. You will fall into Me."

🙏 GUIDED PRAYER

"Lord, help me unplug without unraveling."

God, I confess that unplugging scares me more than I want to admit. I have used entertainment as a shield against my own emotions. I have used distraction as protection from discomfort. I have used digital worlds to quiet the parts of me I didn't know how to confront. But I don't want to rely on escape to survive.

Lord, strengthen me emotionally. Teach me how to sit with my feelings. Teach me how to moderate my appetites. Teach me how to set boundaries without fear. Teach me how to unplug without falling apart. Give me the courage to be present in my own life. Give me the clarity to hear Your voice again. Give me the peace that comes from spiritual stillness. Give me balance, wisdom, and self-control. I surrender the parts of me that have relied on escape. Help me find stability in You, not in stimulation. In Jesus 'name, amen.

REFLECTION PAGE

"What Happens When I Unplug?"
1. **What feelings surface when you disconnect from your escapes?**

____

____

____

____

2. **Which emotions do you fear the most? Why?**

____

____

____

____

____

3. What would emotional stamina look like in your everyday life?

____

____

____

____

4. Where do you need stronger boundaries with entertainment?

____

____

____

____

5. How is God inviting you into balance and moderation?

____

____

____

____

6. What belief have you carried about yourself ("I'm weak," "I can't handle this," etc.) that is not true?

____

____

____

____

____

7.   **What is one small unplug moment you can commit to today?**

____

____

____

____

____

____

____

____

____

____

____

Unplugging will not break you; it will rebuild you.

Chapter 12:

Spiritual Respawn, God Restores What You Logged Out Of

Symptom: When you fear returning to the parts of your life you abandoned.

 You know the feeling, the guilt that hits when you realize you've been logged out of your own purpose for far too long. You didn't intend to drift, disconnect, or disappear. It just happened. Life got heavy. Emotions grew loud. Pressure built quietly. And without knowing the exact moment it began, you withdrew from everything that once made your spirit feel alive. You didn't walk away dramatically; you simply stopped showing up internally. You logged out of your prayer life, your calling, your dreams, your confidence, your discipline, your self-worth, not because you didn't care, but because you didn't feel capable.

The symptom is this: you feel disconnected from the person God created you to be, and you don't know how to reconnect without shame. You want to return, but you fear you're too far gone. You want to pray, but you feel spiritually rusty. You want purpose, but you feel unqualified. You want renewal, but you feel undeserving. You want identity, but you feel like you've forgotten who you are outside of coping, escaping, surviving, or performing.

What you don't realize is that **you never lost your identity, you only lost access to it.** And access can always be restored. Soul-disconnection isn't rebellion; it's overwhelming. Drifting isn't sin; it's fatigue. Logging out isn't rejection of God; it's a response to emotional overload.

And now, standing at the doorstep of return, you fear you can't re-enter the life you left half-lived. But God specializes in spiritual respawns, bringing you back to the place where you stopped believing, stopped fighting, stopped hoping, stopped trusting, and restoring everything that seemed lost.

TEACHING SECTION

"Returning doesn't start with performance, it starts with presence."

There is a lie the enemy loves to whisper: "If you log out spiritually, God logs out too." It's the lie that convinces you restoration requires earning your way back, proving yourself, or starting from zero, as if God has a spiritual scoreboard you ruined by drifting. But that is not how grace works. That is not how God works. That is not how restoration works.

In games, respawning means starting from your last checkpoint. With God, respawning means starting from His mercy, which never resets to zero. The psychology of spiritual drift is rooted in shame. Shame tells you that the distance between who you are and who God  called you to be is too great to cross. Shame convinces you that the time you spent "offline" is irredeemable. Shame tells you've fallen too far, too long, too deep. Shame says restoration is too costly. And because shame is loud, you retreat further into escape.

But the truth is this: God does not restore like humans; He restores like heaven. He doesn't ask, "Where have you been?" He asks, "Are you ready to come home?"

The process of returning to God, the respawn of your spirit, is less about fixing everything and more about allowing Him to touch what you've been afraid to face. It's surrender, not struggle. It's honesty, not performance. It's presence, not perfection.

Spirituals respawn is about reclaiming the parts of your identity you abandoned:

• The strength you traded for survival
• The confidence you exchanged for avoidance
• The vision you replaced with distraction

• The calling you muted
• The voice you silenced
• The peace you forfeited
• The relationship with God you paused

Returning is not about recreating who you were, it's about becoming who you were always meant to be. There is no version of you God is more eager to restore than the one who feels unworthy to return.

℞ FAITH PRESCRIPTION

"Return in small rhythms, not dramatic resets."

1. Begin with one daily return practice.
• A whispered prayer
• A scripture before bed
• A five-minute moment of silence
• A simple "God, I'm here" Consistency > intensity.

2. Identify one area of your calling you abandoned.
Not all. Just one. Ask God: "Where do You want me to start again?"

3. Undo spiritual perfectionism.
You don't need to:
• feel on fire
• know all the verses
• pray eloquently
• "catch up spiritually" Just show up.

4. Practice the 3 R's:
• **Recognize** where you drifted
• **Return** without shame
• **Rebuild** slowly

5. Create a "respawn list."
Write down things God is reviving in you:
• courage
• identity
• discipline
• purpose
• desire for Him
• emotional strength
• hope Highlight one daily.

6. End each day with this confession:
"God restores what I thought I ruined." Your return is not fragile, it's divinely supported.

♻ HOLY SPIRIT CONSULT

"I never logged out of you, I've been waiting for you to log back in."

If the Holy Spirit could speak directly into the quiet place where you feel disconnected, lost, or guilty, He would whisper:"I saw every moment when life overwhelmed you. I saw the nights when numbness felt safer than prayer. I saw the days when you had no strength left to show up spiritually. I did not leave. I did not withdraw. I did not shut down access. I held your identity in My hands while you figured out how to breathe." He would continue with tenderness and authority: "You have not disappointed Me, you have misunderstood Me. I restore quickly. I redeem completely. I revive gently. You don't have to claw your way back to Me. One honest breath brings you into My presence again. You are not returning to punishment; you are returning to love."

Then He would declare: What you logged out of, I preserved. What you abandoned, I protected. What you forgot, I remembered. What you lost, I stored. What you surrendered, I will restore. You are not behind; you are being rebuilt." This is not a comeback; it is a resurrection.

🙏 GUIDED PRAYER

"Lord, help me return to myself and to You."
Father, I come to You with honesty. I admit I've logged out, not because I didn't love You, but because I didn't know how to carry everything I was feeling. Life overwhelmed me. Fear silenced me. Disappointment drained me. Shame convinced me I couldn't return. But today, I laid all of that down.

Lord, restore my identity. Restore my calling. Restore my presence. Restore my desire for You. Restore the parts of me I abandoned out of fear and exhaustion.

I surrender my distance, my numbness, my avoidance, my drift. Give me the courage to return daily, gently, consistently. Give me strength to rebuild. Give me grace to begin again. I choose connection over escape. I choose presence over numbness. I choose purpose over passivity. I choose You over everything else. In Jesus ' name, amen.

REFLECTION PAGE

"Where Do I Need a Spiritual Respawn?"
1. **What part of your life or calling did you quietly log out of? Why?**

____

____

____

____

2.   Which emotion has made returning feel difficult? Fear? Shame? Fatigue? Guilt?

____

____

____

____

____

3.   Where do you feel God tugging you to come back?

____

____

____

____

4.   What spiritual rhythm can you restart today, even in a small way?

____

____

____

____

5.   What lie have you believed about returning to God?

____

____

____

____

____

6. **What truth from this chapter gives you peace or clarity?**

____

____

____

____

7. **What identity is God restoring in you right now?**

____

____

____

____

____

____

____

Return gently. Return consistently. Return without shame. You respawn has already begun.

Chapter 13:

The Real Achievement System, Obedience, Discipline, Healing

SYMPTOM: When your spiritual life has no XP because you never stay long enough to grow.

There's a moment in life when you realize you've mastered leveling up everywhere… except where it matters. You know how to grind in games, how to chase achievements, how to optimize performance, how to build skill sets, how to unlock new abilities, but when it comes to spiritual growth, emotional health, discipline, or obedience, suddenly you feel unmotivated, overwhelmed, or uninterested. You chase consistency in digital worlds but can't seem to sustain it on your own.

This is the symptom: you want transformation, but you don't want the habits that create it. You want healing, but not honesty that initiates it. You want discipline, but not the discomfort that builds it. You want to break through, but not the boundaries that protect it. You want spiritual maturity, but not the daily practices that develop it. You're not sabotaging your life; you're stuck in a cycle where emotional exhaustion meets spiritual avoidance. You keep asking God for change but change never sticks because it's not built on habit, it's built on temporary inspiration. You feel spiritually stagnant not because God isn't moving, but because you're not consistently showing up to the places where growth happens.

You've been conditioned to expect achievement without endurance, reward without repetition, results without routine. Digital systems taught you that consistency is optional, because in gaming, you can always pause, rewind, restart, or respawn. But life? Life requires what a controller never taught you: discipline and obedience are the true XP system of the soul.

TEACHING, "Consistency grows what prayer awakens."

Transformation is not magic; it is the natural outcome of obedience and discipline repeated over time. But because your brain is trained for instant reward systems, you subconsciously expect spiritual and emotional growth to operate the same way. When it doesn't, you assume something is wrong with you. Nothing is wrong, you just haven't trained your habits.

Games reward you every few minutes with dopamine hits. Life rewards you after seasons of consistency. Games give you knew skills instantly. Life requires repetition before mastery. Games celebrate small achievements with sound effects. Life expects you to celebrate progress silently. Games show you a progress bar. Life expects you to trust you're growing even when you can't see it.

This is why discipline feels painful; your brain isn't used to delayed reward. This is why obedience feels inconvenient. Your impulses prefer comfort over responsibility. This is why healing feels slow; your emotions have never been practiced staying present long enough to process. Healing isn't hard, staying  consistent is. Discipline isn't impossible, your habits just aren't trained. Obedience isn't heavy, your priorities are just scattered.

The truth is this: You are not lacking motivation; you are lacking rhythm. You are not spiritually weak; you are spiritually unconditioned. You are not emotionally incapable; you are emotionally underdeveloped because escape steals your practice.

There is a reason God emphasizes *daily* bread, *daily* prayer, *daily* surrender, *daily* obedience, because transformation happens one consistent moment at a time. You cannot microwave spiritual maturity. You cannot speedrun healing. You cannot rush obedience. You cannot cheat-code discipline. You cannot shortcut growth.

God is not waiting for you to be perfect; He is waiting for you to be **consistent**. Consistency is what turns prayer into power.

Consistency is what turns vulnerability into healing. Consistency is what turns scripture into strength. Consistency is what turns worship into warfare. Consistency is what turns obedience into transformation. And here is the supernatural truth: Obedience unlocks what emotion can't. Discipline builds what desire won't. Healing grows where habits sustain it.

💊 FAITH PRESCRIPTION

"Build one life-changing habit at a time."

1. Choose one spiritual habit to master for the next 30 days.
• prayer
• devotion
• journaling
• worship
• silence
• scripture reading
Pick ONE, mastery requires focus.

2. Build a habit stack.
Attach your new habit to something you already do:
• Pray while brushing your teeth
• Worship during your commute
• Read scripture before unlocking your phone
• Journal right after waking up
Your brain learns through pairing.

3. Use the 5-minute rule.
You don't need an hour; you need a start.
Five minutes creates momentum.

4. Celebrate micro-achievements daily.
Don't wait for transformation, celebrate effort.

5. Replace one escape behavior with one grounding behavior daily.

- Anxiety → breathing
- Avoidance → journaling
- Escapism → prayer
- Numbness → worship
- Overthinking → scripture

6. End each day with this confession:

"Obedience is my upgrade. Discipline is my strength. Healing is my reward." Your life changes when your habits change, not before.

✂ HOLY SPIRIT CONSULT

"I strengthen what you bring to Me consistently."

If the Holy Spirit could sit with you while you struggle to build discipline, He would speak gently: I know consistency feels hard for you. I know routine feels overwhelming. I know habits feel impossible when you've spent so long surviving instead of building. But I am not asking you to do this alone. I am here to strengthen what you commit to, not what you perform perfectly." He would continue: When you take one step, I amplify it. When you give Me five minutes, I multiply it. When you show up tired, I refresh you. When you show up discouraged, I reassure you. When you show up inconsistent, I anchor you."

Then He would whisper: You do not grow through will power; you grow through surrender. You do not transform through pressure; you transform through presence.

You do not heal through striving; you heal through obedience." The Holy Spirit is not asking for perfection, He is asking for access.

🙏 GUIDED PRAYER

"Lord, build discipline, obedience, and healing in me."
Father, I come to You honestly. I struggle with consistency. I desire to change but avoid routine. I want growth but wrestle with discipline. I want healing but I fear the process. I want obedience but battle with my own distractions. But today, I surrender all of that to You. Build discipline in me. Strengthen my habits. From routines that transform me. Teach me how to show up even when I don't feel like it. Help me choose growth over comfort. Help me choose obedience over impulse. Help me choose healing over escape.

I give You my delayed effort, my inconsistency, my excuses, and my emotional fatigue. Replace them with patience, structure, devotion, and spiritual rhythm. I can't change myself, but I trust that You can. In Jesus 'name, amen.

REFLECTION PAGE

"What Do I Need to Build, and Why Haven't I?"
1.   **Which habit would transform your life the most if you committed to it?**

____

____

____

____

2.   **What emotional barrier has kept you from consistency?**

____

____

____

____

3.   **Where do you rely on motivation instead of discipline?**

____

____

____

____

4.   **What spiritual practice do you avoid, and why?**

____

____

____

____

5.   **What identity is God building in you through obedience?**

____

____

____

____

6.   **How can you create a simple daily rhythm that supports growth?**

____

____

____

____

7.   **What truth from this chapter challenged or awakened you?**

____

____

____

____

____

____

____

____

____

____

____

Transformation is not complicated; it is consistent.

Chapter 14:

Lag Spikes In Life, Staying Connected to God When You Feel Disconnected

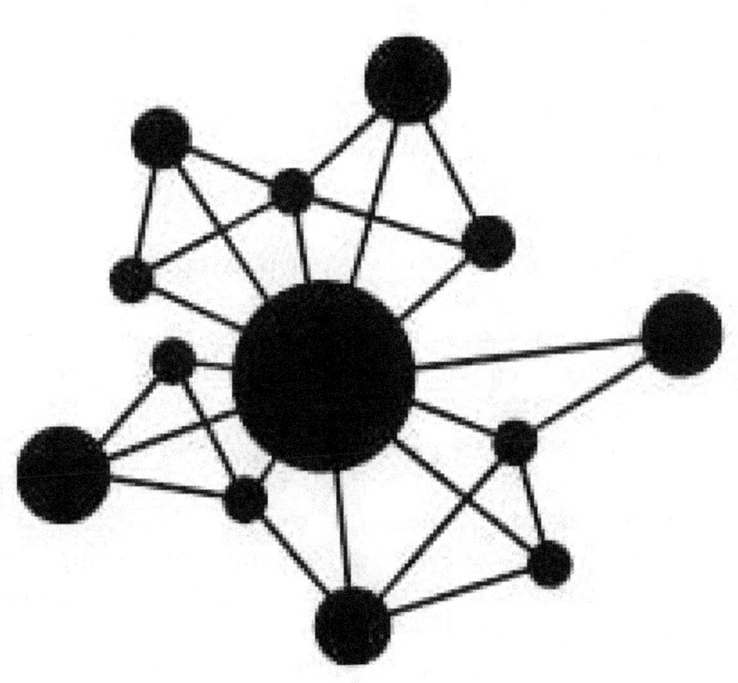

SYMPTOM, When your spirit feels delayed even though God is still present.

 There are moments in your walk with God that feel like a spiritual "lag spike" moments when you pray but don't feel anything, worship but feel numb, read scripture but feel distracted, sit in silence but feel restless. Your mind wanders. Your emotions buffer. Your heart feels half-loaded, like something inside you is stuck between trying to connect and wanting to disconnect.

This is the symptom: you confuse spiritual delay with divine distance. Your emotions slow down, so you assume God stepped back. Your passion fades, so you assume something is wrong with you. Your prayers feel hollow, so you assume God is silent. But what you're really experiencing is spiritual latency, not separation. God didn't disconnect. Your soul did. Not out of rebellion, but out of overload.

Life drains you. Pain distracts you. Stress interrupts your focus. Trauma freezes your emotions. Anxiety fogs your mind. Disappointments weaken your consistency. When the weight gets heavy, your soul does what any system under pressure does, it lags.

The problem is that lag tricks you into believing your spiritual life is malfunctioning. You feel spiritually slow, emotionally dull, mentally unresponsive, and instead of staying connected, you retreat. You assume something is wrong with your relationship with God, when the truth is much simpler: you're trying to feel God through an overwhelmed nervous system. You're not disconnected. You're just delayed. And delay is not death, it's a sign your soul needs support, not shame.

TEACHING, "God is still connected, even when your emotions freeze."

If there is anything gamers understand, it's that lag does not mean the server is down, it means your connection needs strengthening. The same is true spiritually. God doesn't lag. God doesn't buffer. God doesn't lose connection. God doesn't experience technical difficulty. The slowdown isn't on His end, it's on yours. And even then, it's not failure, it's feedback.

Your emotions buffer because your soul is processing more than you realize. Emotional buffering happens when your heart is overloaded with feelings you haven't fully unpacked. Spiritual buffering happens when you're trying to connect with God through layers of exhaustion, distraction, unprocessed pain, stress, fear, or mental clutter. This has nothing to do with holiness, and everything to do with humanity.

You are not spiritually broken. You are spiritually burdened. Lag spikes in life reveal something important: your emotions can slow  your awareness of God's presence, but they cannot slow God's presence itself. Your feelings are not your faith. Your emotions are not your evidence. Your chemistry is not your spirituality. God doesn't disappear when you can't feel Him. God doesn't withdraw when you're overwhelmed. God doesn't punish you with silence when you're numb. God doesn't abandon you because your soul is buffering.

In fact, the moments you feel least connected are often the moments God is doing the most internal work, regulating your emotions, strengthening your endurance, healing your nervous system, pruning your distractions, or inviting you into deeper trust. Spiritual growth requires learning this skill: staying connected even when you don't feel like you're receiving anything. This is the spiritual version of playing through lag, not because you can see everything clearly, but because you trust the connection is still intact.

Your emotions might buffer, but your covenant doesn't. Your feelings might fluctuate, but your faith doesn't have to. Your heart might lag, but your relationship with God remains stable. Lag is frustration, not failure. It is delayed, not distance. It is the soul's version of saying, "Give me a moment, I'm loading."

💊 FAITH PRESCRIPTION

"Stay connected even when your emotions don't catch up."

1. Practice faith actions without requiring faith feelings.
• Pray even when you feel numb.
• Worship even when you feel quiet.
• Read scripture even when it feels dry.
• Sit in silence even when it feels awkward.
Consistency builds connection.

2. Create a "low bandwidth" spiritual routine.
On heavy days, simplify your walk with God:
• One verse
• One prayer
• One breath
• One moment of gratitude
• One surrender
Your soul cannot carry intensity every day, but it can carry consistency.

3. Identify your emotional lag triggers.
• exhaustion
• trauma memories
• relational stress
• anxiety
• overstimulation

• escapism
• disappointment, Awareness reduces shame.

4. Use breath as your "reconnect button."
Inhale: "God, You are here."
Exhale: "Help me stay present."
Your nervous system responds to breath faster than words.

5. Record evidence of God's steadiness weekly.
When you can't feel Him, read what He's already done. Memory builds faith.

🕊 HOLY SPIRIT CONSULT

"Your lag does not scare Me, I stay connected even when you can't."

If the Holy Spirit could speak into your buffering seasons, He would whisper "I haven't gone anywhere. I'm not waiting for you to feel Me to be close to you. My love is not dependent on your emotional signal. I stay connected even when your heart lags, your mind wanders, or your spirit feels tired." He would continue: Do not mistake emotional delay for My distance. I am near even when you are numb. I am speaking even when you are overwhelmed. I am working even when you feel nothing. Your lag is not a sign of rebellion, it is a sign that you need rest, reassurance, and renewal."

Then He would speak with gentle authority: "I sustain you in the silence. I cover you in the buffering. I strengthen you in the delay. I protect you from weakness. You do not maintain this connection, I do. You belong to Me even in the moments you feel unplugged." Your soul may buffer, but God never disconnects.

🙏 GUIDED PRAYER

"Lord, help me stay connected even when I cannot feel You."

Father, I come to You honestly. I feel spiritually slow, emotionally tired, and mentally overwhelmed at times. I admit that I confuse emotional numbness with spiritual distance. But today, I choose trust over interpretation. I choose faith over feelings. I choose connection over confusion.

Lord, steady me. Reconnect with me. Strengthen me. Quiet the noise inside me. Calm the buffering of my emotions. Help me stay consistent even when I feel disconnected. Holy Spirit, remind me that You remain close even when I'm not aware. Help me rest in. Your presence even when it feels silent. Teach me to walk by faith, not by emotional confirmation. Anchor my heart in truth. Restore my sensitivity to Your voice. Renew my awareness of Your nearness. I won't let lag make me leave You. I won't let numbness define my relationship with You. I trust You even when I cannot feel You. In Jesus 'name, amen.

REFLECTION PAGE

"Where Do I Experience Spiritual Lag?"
1. **What emotions buffer most often when you try to connect with God?**

____

____

____

____

2. **Which situations trigger spiritual lag the most (stress, trauma, exhaustion, disappointment)?**

____

____

____

____

3.   What lie do you believe when you feel disconnected from God?

____

____

____

____

4.   What truth from this chapter anchors you?

____

____

____

____

5.   How can you build a low-bandwidth spiritual routine that keeps you consistent?

____

____

---

6.   When was the last time God felt close? What happened?

---

7.   How will you stay connected even during emotional delay?

Your emotions may buffer, but your faith doesn't have to.

Chapter 15:

When Gaming Is Fun Again, Not A Crutch

SYMPTOM, When enjoyment turns into dependency without you noticing.

There was a time when gaming was simply… fun. Lighthearted. Entertaining. Something you did for joy, not survival. But somewhere along the way, the relationship changed. Gaming stopped being a hobby and slowly morphed into a refuge, a place to hide when emotions felt overwhelming, responsibilities felt heavy, or life felt disappointing. It became your buffer, your escape hatch, your emotional oxygen mask. Not because gaming is harmful, but because your heart is hurting.

The symptom now is subtle: you don't know how to enjoy gaming without leaning on it to numb something else. It's not that you don't love playing, you just don't know how to play without losing yourself in it. You don't know how to relax without retreating. You don't know how to have fun without escaping.

Somewhere inside you, joy was replaced by dependence. Recreation turned into medication. And now, ironically, you want your joy back. You want gaming to be enjoyable again, not necessary. You want freedom, not attachment. You want balance, not avoidance. You want recreation, not refuge. But the moment you try to play less, or take a break, or unplug intentionally, something inside your panics. Not because the game is the problem, but because the emotions you've been ignoring resurface the moment the screen dims.

Gaming didn't become your problem; **it became your crutch.** And now you need to learn how to walk again without leaning on it emotionally.

TEACHING, "Recreation is healthy. Escape is hollow. The difference is intention."

One of the biggest misconceptions in healing from escapism is the belief that enjoyment must die for the sake of maturity. But God never asked you to eliminate pleasure, He asked you to stop using pleasure as anesthesia. Recreation is not ungodly. Joy is not immature. Play is not sinful. The problem isn't gaming; it's **why** you game.

Healthy recreation is life-giving, refreshing, balancing. Unhealthy escape is numb, consuming, avoidant. Here's the difference: **Recreation restores your mind. Escape avoids your emotions. Recreation is chosen. Escape is triggered. Recreation adds to your life. Escape distracts you from your life. Recreation is a break. Escape is a hiding place.** When gaming becomes crutch, it stops being enjoyable because it carries the weight of your inner world. It becomes overloaded with responsibility, the responsibility to soothe you, ground you, distract you, stabilize you, and silence your emotional chaos. No hobby was built for that. Even good things collapse under the burden of becoming a substitute for healing.

Healthy recreation requires healthy inner conditions. When you heal internally, your hobbies become joyful externally. When your emotions are processed, your entertainment becomes   balanced. When your soul is steady, your play becomes freedom, not escape. God doesn't want to take gaming from you; He wants to take captivity *out of* your gaming.

You were created to enjoy life without losing yourself in the things meant to bless you. You were created for fun that doesn't compromise your freedom. You were created for recreation that doesn't steal your awareness. You were created for joy that doesn't require emotional withdrawal. Gaming is allowed to be fun again, once you stop needing it to be your hiding place.

💊 FAITH PRESCRIPTION

"Relearn joy, without using it to run from yourself."
<u>1. Play intentionally, not impulsively.</u>
Choose gaming moments on purpose, not automatically. Scheduling joy helps retrain emotional balance.

<u>2. Do an emotional check-in before you play.</u>
Ask:
• Am I escaping or enjoying?
• Am I overwhelmed or just relaxing?
• Am I running from something or resting in something? This builds self-awareness.

<u>3. Set a "joy boundary."</u>
Give gaming a start and end time.
Boundaries protect enjoyment.

<u>4. Add one non-digital joy activity to your week.</u>
• Go outside
• Cook something
• Draw
• Walk
• Listen to worship
• Journal
• Call a friend
Balanced joy builds a balanced soul.

<u>5. Practice "emotional grounding" after you log off.</u>
Sit with yourself for 2–3 minutes. Breathe. Feel. Acknowledge. Reflect. This prevents me from retreating into numbness.

<u>6. End each gaming session with one prayer:</u>

"God, thank You for joy, not escape." You are learning how to enjoy yourself without depending. This is healing.

HOLY SPIRIT CONSULT

"I'm not asking you to stop playing, I'm asking you to stop hiding."

If the Holy Spirit could speak to you as you hold your controller, He would whisper: "I gave you the capacity for joy. I created your imagination. I designed to you to enjoy life. I'm not upset that you love games, I'm concerned that you've been using them to hide from the things I want to heal." He would continue: "I do not want to remove joy from your life. I want to restore balance to your soul. I'm not trying to take away your entertainment; I'm trying to take away the emotional burdens you've placed on it."

Then He would gently say: "You will enjoy your hobbies more when your heart is whole. You will laugh more freely when your emotions are processed. You will have more fun when you are not carrying secret exhaustion. I want to give you peace that makes your play pure again." And finally: "You don't need to escape when you let Me restore you." Your joy will return, not as a crutch, but as a gift.

GUIDED PRAYER

"Lord, teach me how to enjoy life without using joy to hide."

Father, thank You for creating joy. Thank You for giving me interests, hobbies, imagination, and the ability to have fun. But I also admit that I've used gaming to escape, numb, avoid, and distract myself when life felt overwhelming. I don't want to rely on entertainment to soothe what only You can heal.

Lord, restore balance in me. Heal the places that make me prone to escape. Strengthen the parts of me that fear emotional discomfort. Teach me how to rest without running. Teach me how to enjoy without hiding. Teach me how to play without losing myself. Bring me back to joy, real joy, healthy joy, grounded joy. Show me how to use recreation as a blessing, not a refuge. Help me stay connected to You even when I'm unplugging from everything else. Make my hobbies healthy again. Make my heart whole again. In Jesus 'name, amen.

REFLECTION PAGE

"What Does Healthy Joy Look Like for Me?"
1.   **When did gaming stop being fun and start being a crutch?**

____

____

____

____

2.   **What emotions do I avoid by playing?**

____

____

____

____

3.   **How does my body feel after gaming, relaxed or numb?**

____

____

____

____

4.   What would balance joy look like in my weekly routine?

____

____

____

____

5.   Where is God trying to heal me so that my fun can be free again?

____

____

____

____

6.   What boundaries do I need to protect healthy recreation?

____

____

____

7.   How can I practice joy that builds, not numbs?

170

You're not losing gaming; you're losing the chains attached to it.
And that is freedom.

Chapter 16:

DISCHARGE SUMMARY

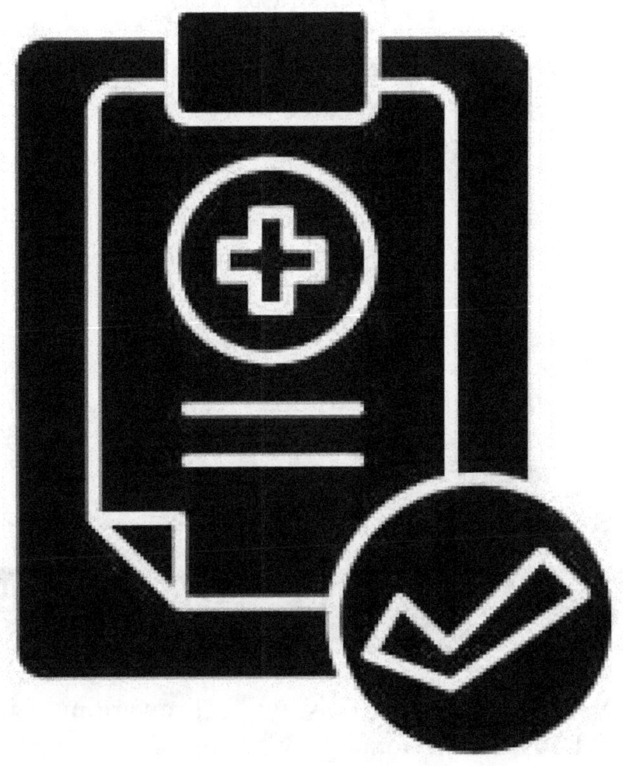

SYMPTOM, When your own life feels like the hardest level you've ever played.

You came into this Clinic because life got loud, overwhelming, confusing, and emotionally tangled. You didn't mean to disappear, you drifted. You didn't mean to escape, you needed relief. You didn't mean to numb out; you were trying to survive emotions that felt too heavy to carry. Games became  grounding, distraction became comfort, avoidance became your rhythm, and escape became your strategy.

But the symptom underneath all of that was this: you forgot that your real life is the story you were created to live in, not the one you were running from. You forgot that purpose still belongs to you. You forgot that God still has plans for you. You forgot that healing is possible for you. You forgot that presence is still inside you. You forgot that strength hasn't left you. You forgot that your life, your actual life, is worth logging back into.

And now, standing at the door of discharge, healed, aware, strengthened, awakened, and spiritually respawned, you're realizing something powerful: God didn't bring you through these chapters to teach you how to escape better. He brought you here to teach you how to live again.

TEACHING, "You were never meant to live logged out of your own story."

Let's be honest: reality doesn't always feel rewarding. Life doesn't hand out XP boosts. Emotional growth doesn't play victory music. Healing doesn't unlock new skill trees overnight. And spiritual disciplines don't come with glowing achievement badges. That's why you drifted. Not because you don't love God. Not because you don't care about your life. But because everything in life that matters requires effort without instant reward. But here's the truth the Holy Spirit has been whispering this entire book: You are not weak, you are overburdened. You are not broken up, you were overloaded. You are not addicted; you were escaping pain you didn't know how to name. You are not spiritually dead; you were spiritually drained.

This Clinic didn't teach you to eliminate joy. It taught you to eliminate *dependence*. This Clinic didn't teach you to fear fun. It taught you to stop using fun as a bandage. This Clinic didn't teach you to abandon gaming. It taught you how to stop abandoning yourself.

Now the shift is beginning, the real achievement system has loaded: Presence over performance. Connection over control. Healing over hiding. Discipline over impulse. Purpose over passivity. Joy over escapism. Life over avoidance.

You are not being discharged back into chaos, you are being discharged into clarity. You are not returning to the life that broke you, you are returning as the healed, aware, strengthened version God rebuilt through these chapters. Your real life is waiting for you, not as an enemy, but as an assignment. Not as a burden, but as a calling. Not as a threat, but as a home.

🔖 FAITH PRESCRIPTION, "Live logged in. Choose presence daily."

<u>1. Maintain the emotional stamina you built.</u>
Sit with your feelings instead of escaping from them.

<u>2. Keep the habits that grounded you.</u>
Five-minute prayer.
Breathwork.
Scripture meditation.

Journaling.
Silence.
Consistency over intensity, always.

3. Use gaming as recreation, never refuge.
If your heart hurts, don't run to a screen.
Run to God.
Run to honesty.
Run to connection.
Then play freely, not fearfully.

4. Schedule weekly "Return to Reality" check-ins.
Ask yourself:
"What am I avoiding?"
"What am I escaping from?"
"What needs attention?"
Healing thrives in honesty.

5. Build a life you don't feel the need to run from.
Limit emotional clutter.
Protect your peace.
Strengthen your relationships.
Feed your spirit.
Choose things that expand you not empty you.

6. End each day with:
"Lord, keep me logged into my life."

🕊 HOLY SPIRIT CONSULT

"I rebuilt what fear convinced you was impossible."

If the Holy Spirit could hand you your discharge papers personally, He would look you straight in the eyes and say: "You did not come here to learn how to fix yourself, you came so I could heal you. You came exhausted, numb, disconnected, overwhelmed, and unsure of who you were becoming. And I took every piece of you, even the ones you were ashamed of, and breathed life back into them."

He would continue: " You are not leaving this Clinic empty. You are leaving empowered. You are not leaving fragile. You are leaving fortified. You are not leaving uncertain. You are leaving aligned."

Then He would whisper with overwhelming tenderness: "You can log back into your life without fear because I go with you. You can face your purpose because I will strengthen you. You can return to the parts of your story you abandoned because I have healed what once made you hide." And finally: "You're ready. Not because you're perfect, but because you're *connected*."

🙏 GUIDED PRAYER

"Lord, help me live fully present."

Father, thank You for every moment of healing You've done in me through this journey. Thank You for restoring my soul, awakening my spirit, strengthening my identity, and teaching me how to stop running from myself. Today I ask for the courage to stay present in my own life.

Lord, help me choose connection over escape. Help me choose healing over avoidance. Help me choose discipline over distraction. Help me choose joy over numbness. Help me choose You over everything that competes for my attention. Give me emotional strength. Give me spiritual stability. Give me clarity, focus, and conviction. Help me live fully logged into the life You designed for me. I'm ready to return, healed, aware, and connected. In Jesus ' name, amen.

REFLECTION PAGE

"What Am I Logging Back Into?"
    1.   **What part of your life are you most ready to return to?**

____

____

____

____

    2.   **What habit of this Clinic has helped you the most?**

____

____

____

    3.   **Where do you feel the Holy Spirit is calling you next?**

____

____

____

____

    4.   **Which emotional patterns do you want to guard against?**

____

____

____

____

____

5. **How will you use gaming in a healthy, balanced way moving forward?**

____

____

____

____

6. **What truth from this book changed your self-awareness the most?**

____

____

____

7. **What are you excited to rebuild in your life?**

____

____

____

You are not returning the same way you left. You are returning renewed.

PERSONAL NOTES

📄 FINAL DISCHARGE INSTRUCTIONS

"Player One, welcome back to your life."

✓ **Keep your emotional bandwidth clear.**

Don't overload your mind, pace yourself.

✓ **Stay plugged into God, even when your emotions lag.**

Your faith is your connection, not your feelings.

✓ **Use gaming as joy, not anesthesia.**

Healthy fun strengthens you, not drains you.

✓ **Return to purpose one step at a time.**

Small obedience builds big transformation.

✓ **Follow up in 30 days for your "Spiritual Maintenance Check."**

Healing is a journey, not a one-time patch update.

✓ **And remember:**

You are free. You are restored. You are reconnected. You are back online. You are ready.

Reflections

____

____

____

____

▦ THE 30-DAY RESET PLAN

"Rebuild Your Life One Day at a Time, Presence Over Escape."
This 30-day plan is structured like a spiritual and emotional respawn cycle, simple, doable, consistent, and transformative. Every day builds on the last. No pressure. No perfection. Just steady progress toward a life you no longer need to escape.

WEEK 1: RECONNECT (Days 1–7)
Goal: Restore awareness, regulate emotions, and return to presence.
Day 1: 5-minute prayer. Tell God honestly, "I'm here."
Day 2: One scripture. One sentence about what it means to you.
Day 3: Breath reset: Inhale "God is near," exhale "I release fear."
Day 4: Emotional check-in: Name what you feel without judging it.
Day 5: Limit gaming by 10%. Create space for awareness.
Day 6: Do something grounding: go outside, stretch, stretch, stretch, journal, sit in silence.
Day 7: Gratitude list of 5 things, even small ones.
Theme: You are rebuilding emotional and spiritual signal strength.

WEEK 2: REPAIR (Days 8–14)
Goal: Confront avoidance, strengthen emotional stamina, rebuild inner structure.
Day 8: Ask yourself: "What emotion am I avoiding?" Write it down.
Day 9: Sit with one feeling for 90 seconds before escaping.
Day 10: Replace one gaming session with a 10-minute worship session.
Day 11: One honest prayer about something real, not polished.
Day 12: Create a boundary: choose one "no gaming after___" time.
Day 13: Check your heart: "What did I run from today?"
Day 14: Sabbath moment, rest without distraction.
Theme: You are repairing the places escape once occupied.

WEEK 3: REBUILD (Days 15–21)

Goal: Build disciplined habits, increase emotional strength, reduce dependence.
Day 15: Pick one habit to master (prayer, journaling, scripture).
Day 16: Attach that habit to something you already do (habit stacking).
Day 17: Play intentionally, not impulsively. Schedule joy.
Day 18: End every gaming session with a grounding check-in.
Day 19: Practice silence for 3 minutes. Let your brain breathe.
Day 20: Choose one responsibility you've been avoiding. Complete it.
Day 21: Celebrate your progress, spiritually, emotionally, mentally.
Theme: Growth comes from rhythm, not intensity.

<u>WEEK 4: RECLAIM (Days 22–30)</u>
Goal: Step fully into the life God restored, without guilt or fear.
Day 22: Pray: "Lord, help me live the life I logged out of."
Day 23: Do something brave, even a tiny step counts.
Day 24: Plan healthy joy: a walk, a conversation, a hobby outside screens.
Day 25: Meditate on your identity: "I am capable. I am whole. I am connected."
Day 26: Evaluate gaming: "Is this fun or escape?" Adjust accordingly.
Day 27: Recommit to one spiritual discipline.
Day 28: Write the biggest thing God healed this month.
Day 29: Declare aloud: "Escape is no longer my refuge God is."
Day 30: Celebrate your reset. Journal your transformation. You did not just regain control, you regained **yourself**.
Theme: This is not just recovery, it is resurrection.

✿ FINAL READER BLESSING

"Player One: Go Live the Story Heaven Wrote for You."
May the Lord bless the parts of you that once felt too tired to show up. May He strengthen the places where escape once felt safer than

truth. May He breathe life into the version of you that didn't think returning was possible. May He restore every fragment of identity you abandoned while trying to survive. I bless your spirit with courage, the courage to live awake, present, grounded, and connected. I bless your mind with clarity, clarity that cuts through confusion, shame, fear, and emotional noise. I bless your heart with balance, the ability to enjoy life without losing yourself inside it. I bless your soul with rest, rest that is holy, restorative, and unforced. May the Holy Spirit remind you daily that you are not fragile, you were simply healing. You are not inconsistent, you were overwhelmed.

*You are not broken, you are rebuilding. You are not behind, you are becoming. May the God of peace be your anchor, May the God of joy be your strength, May the God of wisdom be your guide, May the God of healing be your home. Go live your life, fully logged in, fully alive, fully present. Your story is waiting. Your purpose is to wait. Your joy is waiting. Your future is waiting. You are free. You are restored. You are ready. **Now go, Player One. Your life is loading.***

▨ BEST-SELLER CONCLUSION

"You Didn't Just Finish a Book, You Reclaimed Your Life."

If you are reading these final pages, it means you've done something most people never do in their entire lives, you turned around and faced the very things you used to run from. You unmasked your escape habits. You confronted your emotional exhaustion. You told the truth about your digital dependencies. You explored your numbness, your fear, your avoidance, your drift, your distractions, and the quiet places inside you that felt easier to ignore than to heal. You didn't come to this Clinic because you were weak, you came because you were *done* pretending. You were tired of hiding in fictional worlds while your real one begged for your presence. You were tired of logging into games and logging out of your own story. You were tired of feeling connected online but disconnected inside your own soul. You were tired of walking through life like a ghost with a pulse.

This book wasn't just teaching. It wasn't just therapy language. It wasn't just metaphor. It was your wake-up call. Your turning point. Your respawn moment. Your spiritual reboot. And here's the truth you discovered somewhere between Chapter One and Chapter Sixteen: You were never addicted to gaming; you were addicted to escaping the version of you that believed you weren't enough. But now you know better. Now you know that you can feel without falling apart.

Now you know that you can unplug without unraveling. Now you know that you can face your life without fear swallowing you whole. Now you know that joy doesn't have to replace healing, it can coexist with it. Now you know that balance isn't impossible, it's intentional. Now you know that your emotions won't destroy you, they're only information. And now, most importantly, you know this: God never saw you as someone who needed to escape. He saw you as someone worth rescuing. What you thought was weakness was weariness. What you thought was laziness was overwhelm. What you thought was distance was buffering. What you thought was failure was a soul crying out for restoration.

You didn't just heal from escapism; you healed from the lies that made you want to escape in the first place. And now you stand here, not at the end of a book, but at the beginning of a life you no longer fear stepping into. You are not the same person who downloaded this. You are not the same soul who walked into this Clinic. You are not the same heart that hid behind screens. You left every chapter changed, subtly, powerfully, permanently.

You learned how to confront instead of retreat. You learned how to feel instead of numb. You learned how to pray instead of panic. You learned how to reconnect instead of escape. You learned that healing doesn't have to be loud, sometimes it sounds like a quiet "Yes" whispered in God's direction. And even now, as you close this final chapter... something inside you knows the truth: You are not going back to who you were. You can't. You've grown too much. You've woken up too deeply. You've healed too honestly. This is not the end. This is your **re-entry**.

Welcome back to your own story, the one God wrote for you, the one the enemy tried to distract you from, the one trauma tried to silence, the one escapism tried to overshadow, the one numbness tried to erase.

But here you are. Awake. Present. Healed. Aware. Reconnected. Restored.

This is your final achievement: You logged back into your life. And you're not logging out again. Now go live boldly. Go live fully. Go live free. Go live with intention. Go live with joy. Go live with balance. Go live with God, not as your last resort, but as your first response.

Your story is waiting for your courage. Your dreams are waiting for your discipline. Your healing is waiting for your consistency. Your purpose is to wait for your presence.

And heaven is cheering you on.

Player One, Your life is loading, and this time… you're ready!

PERSONAL NOTES

ABOUT THE AUTHOR

Dr. Patricia Tanner was born and raised in Sanford FL. She comes from a family of three siblings. Patricia Tanner is the founder of Multhai International Realty, Multhai Asset Management Services, and Multhai Investment Group which is located in Sanford, Florida. She is a graduate of the University of Central Florida, where she received a Bachelor of Science in Business Administration and a minor in Human Resources Management.

Dr. Tanner began her career shortly thereafter as a Regional Property Manager in the apartment community. Throughout her career in property management, she has built interpersonal relationships with corporate clients. She has a successful track record of increasing company revenues over $5 million annually, through hard work, commitment, creativeness, and strategic planning.

Her experience and leadership role eventually led her to achieve a Florida Real Estate Broker license. She spent fifteen years in the Real Estate field while completing a Master of Arts in Human Resources Management from Webster University, and a Master of Public Administration from Troy University. It was in this capacity that she decided to open her own brokerage company, Multhai International Realty.

In addition, Dr. Tanner finds time in her busy schedule to participate in her own Non-For-Profit Organization, Stones 2 Homes. She remains President of her organization in which she helps people build, keep, or purchase homes in affordable communities. She is the founder of PNT Property Partners in which she buys vacant land, develops it, and constructs brand new construction homes in Sanford Florida. Her overall goal is to educate and provide resources to help people overcome financial hardships and credit disadvantage to live the American Dream through homeownership in spite of economic hardship. Through her visions she will continue to grow as an entrepreneur and is willing to share her knowledge, experience, and expertise with anyone who is willing to learn.

MORE BOOKS BY THE AUTHOR

Welcome to the Faith Clinic—where your soul doesn't need to be perfect to be healed.

You've smiled through burnout. Quoted scripture while quietly unraveling. Prayed, fasted, and still felt like your faith flatlined. If that's you, Faith Clinic: Volume I is your spiritual prescription.

Dr. Patricia S. Tanner—known as The Faith Doctor—invites you into a raw, grace-filled recovery journey for the soul. With 7 powerful doses of faith-infused wisdom, this book delivers healing where performance failed and offers truth where church hurt left a scar. Designed especially for spiritually exhausted youth and young adults, each "dose" reads like an IV drip of hope for believers secretly running on empty.

You don't need to be okay to show up. You just need to be willing. The clinic is open.

NOW AVAILABLE:
www.amazon.com

Healing was just the beginning. Now it's time to grow.

If Faith Clinic Volume I met you in crisis, Volume II meets you in recovery. Because faith isn't a one-time fix—it's a lifestyle that needs maintenance, accountability, and consistency. Welcome to your follow-up care plan.

In Faith Clinic: Volume II, Dr. Patricia S. Tanner—aka The Faith Doctor—guides you through the next level of your spiritual healing journey. From navigating church trauma and burnout to facing silence from God and rediscovering purpose, this book goes deeper than devotionals. It's not about hype—it's about habits that sustain real, lasting transformation.

With raw wisdom, relatable stories, and no-shame truths, each chapter is a spiritual check-in for believers who want to thrive—not just survive. Whether you're wrestling with doubt, craving stability, or simply ready to grow up in God, this clinic is for you.

You've detoxed. Now it's time to build. Let's get you discharge-ready.

NOW AVAILABLE:
www.amazon.com

Welcome to the Faith Clinic: Anxiety Edition — where God doesn't coddle your coping mechanisms but confronts them with surgical precision.

This book is for the ones who love Jesus but still can't sleep. For the worship leaders crying in church bathrooms. For the believers who pray in spirals, fight shame on Sundays, and secretly think, "Maybe I'm the only one who can't seem to breathe through this." You're not crazy. You're just in a fight — and this book is your spiritual triage.

Inside you'll find:
- Panic attacks in pews and the prayers that still work.
- Scriptures that talk you off the ledge.
- What to do when you feel numb and God feels quiet.
- How to walk out of shame loops, judgment spirals, and performance religion.

This isn't just encouragement. It's equipment.
Because healing isn't a moment — it's a walk.

NOW AVAILABLE:

www.amazon.com

Welcome to the Faith Clinic: Stress Edition — where we don't hand you cute verses and clichés. We hand you spiritual prescriptions for real pressure, real panic, and real prayers from tired believers holding it together by a thread.

This book is for the overwhelmed—those trusting God while juggling bills, burnout, hustle culture, and holy frustration. If you've ever whispered, "God, are You even watching this mess?" this is for you.

Inside you'll find raw, soul-hitting chapters like:

- "God, I Trust You — But These Bills Keep Coming"
- "If Rest Is Holy, Why Does It Feel Like Slacking?"
- "I'm Tired of Smiling So You Won't Worry"

This isn't fluff. It's real talk for real stress—and a reminder that you're not forgotten, you're being fortified.

The Faith Clinic is open. Breathe in & take your spiritual vitamins. Healing begins here.

NOW AVAILABLE:

www.amazon.com

This isn't just a feeling — it's a flare signal from the soul. You pray, serve, and believe in God, but something deep inside is still simmering. Welcome to the Faith Clinic: Anger Edition — where suppressed emotions meet sacred intervention.

In this volume, Dr. Patricia S. Tanner guides you through spiritual triage for:

- ☑ Silent rage and emotional suppression
- ☑ The grief–anger connection
- ☑ Rejection wounds from childhood to church hurt

This isn't a lecture. It's a spiritual detox. No shame. No sugarcoating. Just raw, honest healing. Whether you're snapping at loved ones or silently seething under the surface, this book meets you at the boiling point—and leads you to the breakthrough.

🩺 This is the clinic.

🔥 This is your moment.

And God is ready to heal the anger behind your amen.

NOW AVAILABLE:

www.amazon.com

In this powerful installment of the Faith Clinic series, Dr. Patricia S. Tanner brings biblical insight, emotional compassion, and spiritual strength to those walking through grief. Designed as a healing chamber for the soul, each "dose" of this devotional targets a different dimension of sorrow—guiding you from pain to peace, from mourning to joy.

Inside, you'll discover:

- Daily doses of Scripture-based encouragement.
- Personal reflections and prayers for each stage of grief.
- Practical faith prescriptions to help you process loss and find purpose.

Whether you are navigating the recent loss of a loved one, confronting buried grief from the past, or supporting someone else in their sorrow, this devotional offers a gentle yet powerful roadmap to healing. Come, take your seat in the Faith Clinic—where the Great Physician is ready to restore your soul.

NOW AVAILABLE:

www.amazon.com

30 Days Of Grieving

Given By The Inspiration Of God

Healing From COVID-19

Almost a year later, it hit me... My mother was gone, and I was still stuck at the hospital. I had tried everything from crying to counseling, and even prayer. Pray they told me. Trust God they insisted. But it seemed as if nothing was working. I was hurt, dealing with my reality: my mother was not coming back.

While journeying through grief, it was under the divine 'Inspiration of God' that He placed me in a trance. While I was gaining a revelation about grief, He gave me this journal, '30 Days Of Grieving.'

NOW AVAILABLE:

www.amazon.com

The 30 Days Challenge:

I Tested POSITIVE for COVID-19

If you had 30 days to live, what would you do? If you were told that you needed to prepare for a marathon in 30 days and you were completely out of shape, what would you do first? If a family member handed you one million dollars and told you that you had to figure out how to build a house (debt free), how would you execute your plan?

I'm catching you off guard with these requests, right? Well, this is exactly what COVID-19 did when it snatched my mother's life away, wrecking my entire world. I had to battle for my mother AND my faith in 30 days flat. What a challenge!

Throughout this book, I will walk you through my brief journey with COVID-19, negative of a happy ending. I will share the diary I kept while attending to my mother, and the scriptures I read, prayed, and quoted as my shield and protection.

Take the journey with me, there is healing on the other side!

NOW AVAILABLE:

www.amazon.com

Can Salvation Get You Into Heaven? The Answer Is Yes! offers a powerful and biblically grounded exploration of God's eternal plan, revealing the heart of the Gospel and the assurance of salvation through Jesus Christ.

 Unpacking life's most vital questions—Who is God? Why were we created? What does Jesus' life mean for us?—this book brings clarity to the believer's journey and confirms that salvation, once received, is eternally secure.

Whether you're seeking understanding or affirming your faith, this inspiring guide will lead you into the confidence and joy of knowing heaven is your eternal home.

NOW AVAILABLE:
www.amazon.com

The Bench That Waited is a bold and prophetic call to action for believers who've grown comfortable in church attendance but stagnant in purpose.

With raw honesty and spiritual insight, Patricia Tanner exposes the quiet crisis of passive faith—where callings are delayed and obedience is optional.

Through Scripture, stories, and reflection, this book urges readers to rise from routine, break free from spiritual stagnation, and step boldly into their Kingdom assignment. The bench has waited long enough—will you?

NOW AVAILABLE:

www.amazon.com

What happens when the Kingdom becomes a stranger?

The Godless Climb is not a rejection of faith—it is a raw, unflinching journey through what remains when belief unravels. With brutal honesty and tender grace, this book explores the spiritual free fall that follows the loss of divine certainty, the ache of unanswered prayers, and the void left when God no longer feels near.

Written for those who have quietly slipped out of the pews and into a wilderness of doubt, grief, and inner searching, this is not a triumph story—but a survival story. A confession. A sacred wrestle. Through personal reflection and prophetic insight, the author unpacks what it means to climb without a safety net, to live without the scaffolding of religious performance, and to build a new compass in the absence of old crutches.

You haven't arrived. But you're still climbing. And that is holy.

NOW AVAILABLE:
www.amazon.com

The Triple 7 Formula is designed for business owners who are looking forward to hitting the million-dollar mark in their business. If you own a business and seem to be running in financial circles, this book will get you on track to simultaneously gaining sound business structure and millions in your bank account.

It was through many conversations with business owners lacking financial gain that prompted Patricia to share her blueprint for millionaire status. Through this book, she demonstrates how to gain financial ground by developing strong teams, implementing systems, and setting stackable goals. If you are ready to gain a laser sharp focus, and implement these clear steps, you will position yourself for financial greatness. Your business will be sound, and you will see financial growth beyond your wildest dreams!!

NOW AVAILABLE:

www.amazon.com

The Triple 7 Formula is specifically crafted for business owners aspiring to reach the million-dollar milestone. If you are a business owner feeling stuck in financial cycles, this book will set you on the path to building both a solid business structure and financial success.

This workbook is designed to complement the textbook of the same name. As you progress through its pages, you will be inspired to take decisive steps toward becoming a millionaire. From constructing your business framework to creating the millionaire's avatar, this process will expand your knowledge and mindset. Not only will you chart a course to financial success, but you will also identify your accountability circle and select a mentor to guide you toward greatness.

I cannot guarantee millionaire status unless you actively follow the steps to begin your journey. If you are searching for a get rich quick scheme, this workbook is not for you. I am looking for those ready to put in the effort—and since you are reading this, I believe that's you!

You have finally found it: Your roadmap to millions!

NOW AVAILABLE:
WWW.Amazon.com

Find Patricia on The Web:

www.PatriciaTanner.com

Follow Patricia on social media:

Facebook & Instagram: @PatriciaTannerInc

www.ingramcontent.com/pod-product-compliance
Lightning Source LLC
Chambersburg PA
CBHW071618030726
47598CB00001B/330